WORLD WAR II:
THE PACIFIC

Sean Sheehan

W

FRANKLIN WATTS
LONDON•SYDNEY

Titles in this series:

The Arab-Israeli Conflict
The Korean War
The Vietnam War
World War I
World War II: Europe
World War II: The Pacific

© 2004 Arcturus Publishing

Produced for Franklin Watts by Arcturus Publishing Ltd, 26/27 Bickels Yard, 151-153 Bermondsey Street, London SE1 3HA.

Series concept: Alex Woolf
Editor: Philip de Ste. Croix
Designer: Simon Borrough
Cartography: The Map Studio
Consultant: Paul Cornish, Imperial War Museum, London
Picture researcher: Thomas Mitchell

Published in the UK by Franklin Watts.

A CIP catalogue record for this book is available from the British Library.

ISBN 0 7496 5448 1

Printed and bound in Italy

Franklin Watts – the Watts Publishing Group, 96 Leonard Street, London EC2A 4XD.

Picture Acknowledgements:
All the photographs in this book, except for that appearing on page 41, were supplied by Getty Images and are reproduced here with their permission. The photograph on page 41 was taken by Joe Rosenthal and is reproduced courtesy of Popperfoto.

About The Author

The author, Sean Sheehan, is a full-time writer who previously worked as a teacher in London and the Far East. While visiting sites and locations associated with World War II in Singapore and Malaysia, he began to research the history of the war. He is also the author of *Germany and Japan Attack* and *World War II: The Allied Victory* in Hodder Wayland's World Wars series.

CONTENTS

CHAPTER 1:
JAPANESE VICTORIES

Japanese troops parading through the Chinese city of Shanghai, captured in November 1937 after more than four months of fighting.

After many centuries of isolation from most of the world, Japan was well on its way to becoming a modern country by the 1930s. With seventy million people to feed, Japan welcomed Western technology but lacked natural resources, like oil and rubber, which were vital for a modernizing country. Unlike nations such as Britain and France, Japan also lacked an overseas empire in Asia that could provide it with wealth and natural resources. To remedy this, Japan took aggressive action to occupy a region in northern China called Manchuria in 1931 and six years later extended its control by going to war with China. The invasion of China in 1937, however, did not lead to a complete victory.

When World War II started in 1939, it was at first a European war that mainly involved Germany fighting other western European nations. However, the outbreak of war in Europe encouraged those in Japan who

A WAR ECONOMY

During the 1930s, governments in Japan spent more and more on their military build-up. These statistics show Japan developing a war economy.

Military budget as percentage of total government spending:
1931 29 per cent
1932 38 per cent
1933 39 per cent
1934 44 per cent
1935 47 per cent
1936 48 per cent
1937 72 per cent
1938 75 per cent
1939 72 per cent
1940 66 per cent
[From *The Oxford Companion to World War II*, edited by I.C.B. Dear]

saw further military expansion as the only way to make their country rich. By 1941 France and the Netherlands had been defeated by Germany, and Britain seemed powerless to resist. This gave Japan an opportunity to take over the Asian colonies of these weakened European powers. The natural resources of these colonies would enable Japan to defeat China, build up its own empire and stop relying on imports from hostile foreign countries like the USA.

THE UNITED STATES The hostility of the United States was the major stumbling block to Japan's ambitions. Although only the Philippines and a few islands in the Pacific were under American control, the US had its own ambitions in the region. The US particularly wanted to influence events in China, and had

no intention of sharing naval power in the Pacific with Japan. In 1941 Japan began to grow short of essential imports after the US restricted its trade. This economic war got more bitter when Japan moved into the south of French Indo-China. The USA and Britain froze all Japanese funds under their control and cut essential oil supplies to Japan.

Japan had either to back down, by withdrawing from Manchuria, China and French Indo-China, or seize control of the European colonies in Asia and their natural resources. This would bring armed conflict with the US – but one way of dealing with this threat would be to launch a surprise attack on the US Navy and destroy its Pacific fleet.

Admiral Isoroku Yamamoto, the Commander-in-Chief of the Japanese Navy, planned a surprise attack

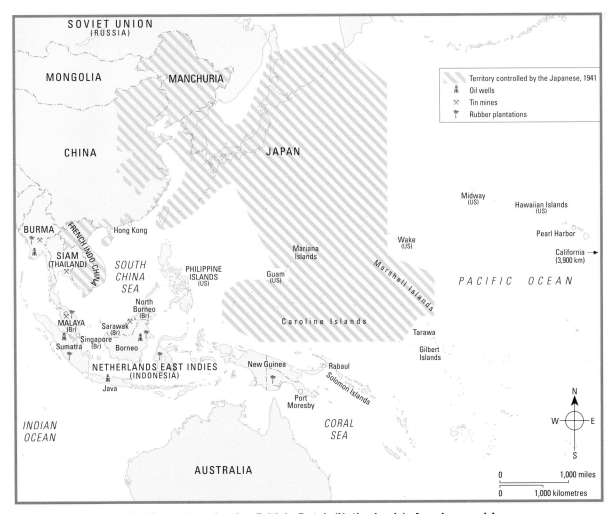

The countries in the Pacific region, showing British, Dutch (Netherlands), American and Japanese possessions, before war broke out in December 1941.

on Hawaii that was meant to destroy the American fleet that had been stationed there since the previous year. 'Climb Mount Niitaka' was the code sent by Yamamoto at the end of November 1941 for six Japanese aircraft carriers to set sail from the north-east of Japan and travel some 6,500 km to Hawaii, maintaining radio silence to avoid detection.

On 7 December, early in the morning, 183 Japanese planes gathered in a V-formation after taking off from the six aircraft carriers to the north of Hawaii. It took them over an hour to reach the island of Oahu, guided to their target by a local radio station playing music. Shortly before 8 am bombs began to rain down on the harbour and airfields. A second wave of attackers arrived at 8.40 am and inflicted more damage. American losses, in total, included eighteen sunk or badly damaged ships, including six battleships, 162 aircraft and the lives of 2,403 servicemen and civilians. The Japanese lost twenty-nine planes and their crews.

US naval power was not destroyed, however, mainly because the three aircraft carriers based at Hawaii were all out at sea at the time of the attack. A third Japanese attack, targeting the harbour's fuel tanks and repair facilities, was called off for fear of a counterattack from the aircraft carriers. If the fuel dumps had been destroyed, Pearl Harbor would have been permanently put out of action.

The US and Japan were now at war. Various claims have been made that advance warning of the attack was kept secret by US President Franklin D. Roosevelt and by Winston Churchill, Britain's wartime leader, because they wanted the United States to go to war. Historians have found no convincing evidence for this. There were intelligence reports indicating that something was to happen on 7 December but no-one put

them together and drew the conclusion that Pearl Harbor was in danger of attack.

Unlike the Americans and Pearl Harbor, the British were expecting the Japanese to attack Malaya

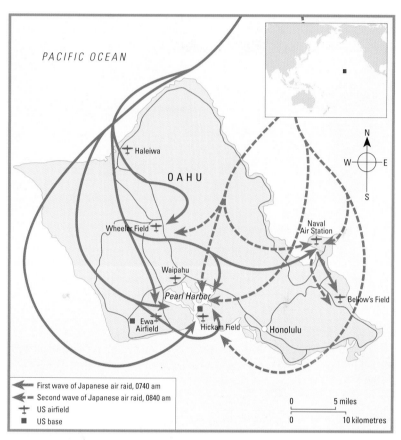

The Japanese bombing of Pearl Harbor was a complete surprise because no-one expected a long-distance attack from the north.

EYE WITNESSES

Leonard J. Fox, writing a letter home on board the USS *Helena* at the time, remembers what he saw on the ground: '*Torpedo planes swooped in from almost over my head and started toward "Battleship Row" dropping their lethal fish [torpedos]. First the* Oklahoma *… then it was the* West Virginia *taking blows in her innards … and now it is the* Arizona *… Men were swimming for their lives in the fire-covered waters of Pearl Harbor.*'

[From *The Pacific Campaign*, Dan Van Der Vat]

US warships in Pearl Harbor proved an easy target because few of their guns were manned and ammunition was locked away.

Japanese forces at the southern tip of the Malayan peninsula.

The Japanese attack on Malaya, planned to begin at exactly the same time as the attack on Pearl Harbor on 7 December 1941, accidentally began a short while earlier. Siam was also attacked.

(W. Malaysia). They knew the Japanese would probably land on the beaches in the border area around north Malaya and south Siam (Thailand). This is what happened shortly after midnight on 8 December 1941. Local time in Hawaii was then 6 am on 7 December – it would be almost two hours before the first wave of planes reached Pearl Harbor – so the landings in south Siam and Malaya were Japan's first aggressive action in the Pacific war.

THE INVASION OF
MALAYA   Waiting for the

Japanese was a large army of British-led troops, mostly Indians but also including Australians. They were continually pushed back as a smaller number of Japanese forces advanced at a blistering pace down the peninsula towards Singapore.

Most of the Japanese forces had no previous experience of jungle warfare but they were battled-hardened from fighting in China. Many of the troops they were fighting were inexperienced, and some of the Indian troops had

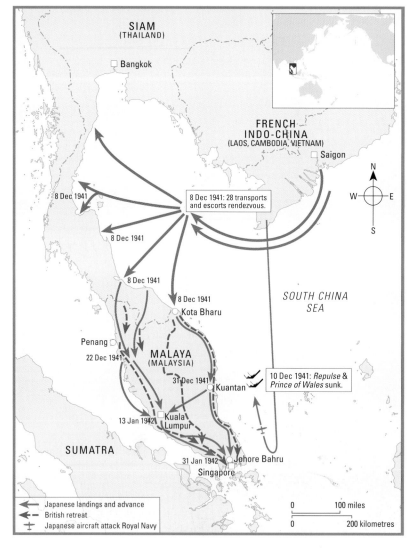

SIAM
(THAILAND)

☐ Bangkok

FRENCH
INDO-CHINA
(LAOS, CAMBODIA, VIETNAM)

☐ Saigon

8 Dec 1941

8 Dec 1941: 28 transports
and escorts rendezvous.

8 Dec 1941

8 Dec 1941

SOUTH CHINA
SEA

8 Dec 1941
○ Kota Bharu

Penang ○

22 Dec 1941

MALAYA
(MALAYSIA)

10 Dec 1941: *Repulse* &
Prince of Wales sunk.

31 Dec 1941

○ Kuantan

13 Jan 1942   ☐ Kuala
Lumpur

SUMATRA

31 Jan 1942   ○ Johore Bahru
Singapore

Japanese landings and advance
British retreat
Japanese aircraft attack Royal Navy

0   100 miles
0   200 kilometres

never seen a tank until faced by some of the eighty transported by the Japanese. The Japanese also brought bicycles to travel down the well-maintained roads, and they used maps copied from school atlases. One Japanese tactic, when faced with enemy resistance, was often to go around the obstacle through the jungle or to use boats to bypass it along the coastline. The Japanese were also able to attack from the air, flying in from Indo-China and attacking British airfields. They quickly gained control of the skies over Malaya.

The defenders were not prepared for the well-trained and experienced Japanese who easily brushed aside attempts to hold them back. In only ten weeks, the Japanese had reached the southern tip of the peninsula. At this point only a narrow stretch of water divided the mainland from the island of Singapore, where the retreating Allied soldiers were now concentrated for a final battle with their enemy.

The islands of the Philippines – which served as a US military base in Asia – were around 11,000 km from the US West Coast, and 8,000 km even from Pearl Harbor, but only 2,000 km from Japan. General Douglas MacArthur, in overall military command of US forces in the Philippines, argued nevertheless

LOSS OF BATTLESHIPS

Two British battleships, HMS *Prince of Wales* and HMS *Repulse*, were dispatched from Singapore to intercept Japanese invasion forces. They were sunk off Malaya's east coast on 10 December 1941 in a land-based air attack; 840 men lost their lives. A war correspondent, O.D. Gallagher, was on the *Repulse*: '... *They were bombers. Flying straight at us. All our guns pour high-explosives at them, including shells so delicately fused that they explode if they merely graze cloth fabric. But they swing away, carrying out a high-powered evasive action without dropping anything at all. I realise now what the purpose of the action was. It was a diversion to occupy all our guns and observers on the air defence platform at the summit of the main mast. There is a heavy explosion and the* Repulse *rocks.'*

[From the *Daily Express*, 12 December 1941]

Before 1941, few thought that battlecruisers like HMS *Repulse* could be sunk from the air.

The controversial General Douglas MacArthur, admired as well as criticized by historians.

Unlike Pearl Harbor, an attack on the Philippines was anticipated but US forces were still defeated.

Japanese General Masaharu Homma sets foot on Philippine soil to oversee the capture of the islands.

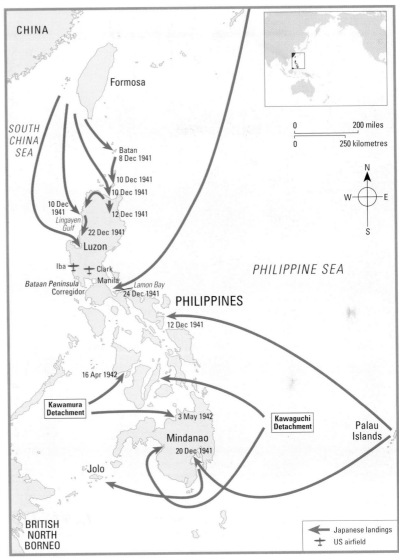

that the islands could be defended and he built up a force of 30,000 American troops and over 100,000 Filipinos. The presence of B-17 bombers and over 100 P-40 fighter aircraft gave the Philippines the largest concentration of US air power in the Pacific.

Over nine hours passed between news of Pearl Harbor first reaching MacArthur's headquarters and the arrival of Japanese attack planes over Luzon. Historians are puzzled why nothing was done during this period, and why the Japanese attack was able to destroy B-17s and P-40s still on the ground at Clark airfield. A squadron of US aircraft, returning from a patrol at the time, was also taken by surprise and wiped out. MacArthur had lost half of his aircraft on the same day, 8 December 1941, that Japanese troops

Japanese soldiers celebrate the capture of a large American gun on Bataan; it took three months before they were finally able to capture the peninsula, early in April 1942.

began landing on Batan island to the north of Luzon.

Smaller landings took place over the next few days but the main Japanese invasion force arrived on 22 December in Lingayen Gulf on the west of Luzon. Two days later, more Japanese landed on the east coast in Lamon Bay and it became clear that General Masaharu Homma, commanding the Japanese, intended to trap the defending forces in a pincer movement. MacArthur, realizing this, decided to withdraw from around the capital city of Manila. Troops were ordered to retreat to the Bataan peninsula while the military command and the Philippine government withdrew to the island of Corregidor, south of the peninsula.

MacArthur needed reinforcements but US military commanders back in Washington D.C. did not want to

BOMBING MANILA

Carlos Romulo was working in Manila on 8 December when Japanese planes suddenly appeared in the sky: *'Fifty-four Japanese sky monsters, flashing silver in the bright noonday, were flying in two magnificently formed Vs. Above the scream of the sirens the church bells solemnly announced the noon hour.*

Unprotected and unprepared, Manila lay under the enemy planes – a city of ancient nunneries and chromium-fronted night clubs, of skyscrapers towering over nipa [palm] shacks, of antiquity and modernity, of East and West.

... Something pressed between my feet. It was Cola, the office cat, her feline instincts alarmed by the sirens. Their screaming stopped, and in their place we heard the throbbing of the planes.'

[Quoted in *How It Happened: World War II*, edited by Jon E. Lewis]

risk further losses at this stage. President Roosevelt told MacArthur to hold on for as long as was possible. A siege of the Bataan peninsula followed, as some 67,000 Filipino troops, over 12,000 Americans and 26,000 civilians squeezed onto a strip of land 40 km long and 32 km wide.

The year 1942 began with the Japanese driving forward into the Netherlands East Indies (Indonesia), the British falling back towards Singapore, and the Americans and Filipinos digging in on the Bataan peninsula.

Japanese troops, under the command of General Masaharu Homma, attacked early in January and broke through around Mt Natib in the Philippines. The US forces withdrew to a final line of defence, between Bagac and Orion, and forced Homma to call a halt to further attacks. The siege that followed lasted over two months.

By the beginning of February all the British-led

British General Arthur Percival (on the extreme right) on his way to sign a formal declaration of the surrender of Singapore in February 1942.

troops were on Singapore island (see page 8) and another, shorter, siege began. With 70,000 soldiers at his disposal, the British general Arthur Percival made the mistake of trying to defend the entire length of Singapore's northern coastline and the Japanese were able to break through. Despite having only 35,000 troops, and with little ammunition left, the Japanese commander, General Tomoyuki Yamashita, waited to see what would happen. The city of Singapore was demoralized, some troops panicked and began to desert, and in the middle of February Percival surrendered to Yamashita. Churchill called it 'the worst disaster and largest capitulation in British history'.

Meanwhile, MacArthur had been instructed to leave Corregidor and seek safety in Australia. The troops he left behind were under orders not to surrender but this became increasingly difficult in view of what was happening. Food was in seriously short supply, malaria and other illnesses afflicted the besieged, and resistance became futile when the Japanese attacked once again in April. The American in charge, Major-General Edward King, disobeyed MacArthur and surrendered on 9 April to save unnecessary deaths. Nearly 80,000 survivors were

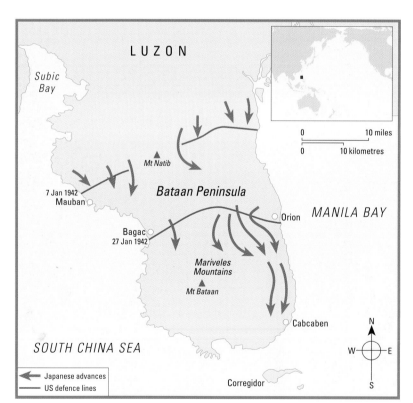

Such was the shortage of food, the defenders on Bataan were reduced to eating horses and water buffalo before surrender to the invading Japanese forces became inevitable.

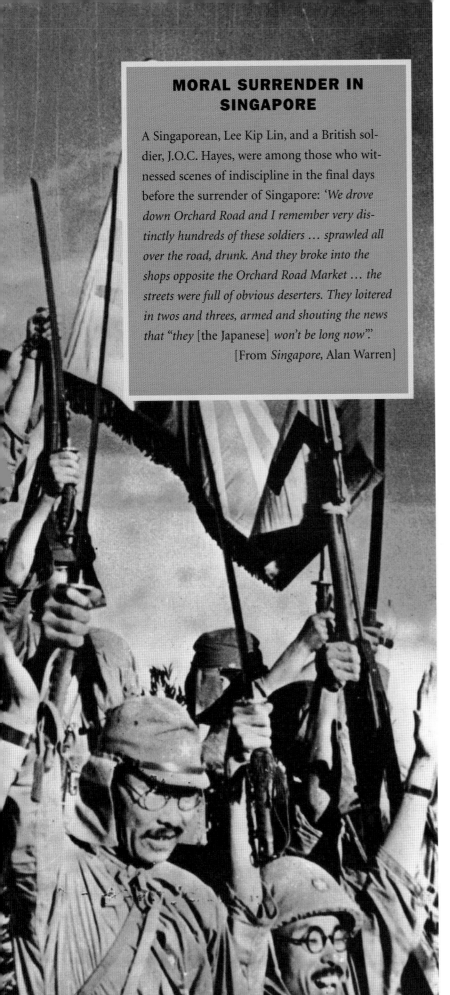

MORAL SURRENDER IN SINGAPORE

A Singaporean, Lee Kip Lin, and a British soldier, J.O.C. Hayes, were among those who witnessed scenes of indiscipline in the final days before the surrender of Singapore: *'We drove down Orchard Road and I remember very distinctly hundreds of these soldiers ... sprawled all over the road, drunk. And they broke into the shops opposite the Orchard Road Market ... the streets were full of obvious deserters. They loitered in twos and threes, armed and shouting the news that "they* [the Japanese] *won't be long now".'*

[From *Singapore*, Alan Warren]

marched out of the peninsula on what became known as the Bataan Death March (see pages 26-7).

THE WAR SPREADS By April 1942, the Japanese had not only conquered Malaya, Singapore and the Philippines, the greater part of the Netherlands East Indies had also been overrun, Hong Kong had surrendered, and the British were also defeated in southern Burma. Japan and the US were at war after the attack on Pearl Harbor and, following the invasion of Malaya, Britain and Japan were also at war. Germany had also declared war on the USA. World War II was now a truly global conflict.

The fortified island of Corregidor finally surrendered on 7 May 1942.

Jubilation breaks out when Japanese soldiers are told that the US and Filipino troops who were defending Bataan have surrendered.

CHAPTER 2:
LAND AND SEA BATTLES

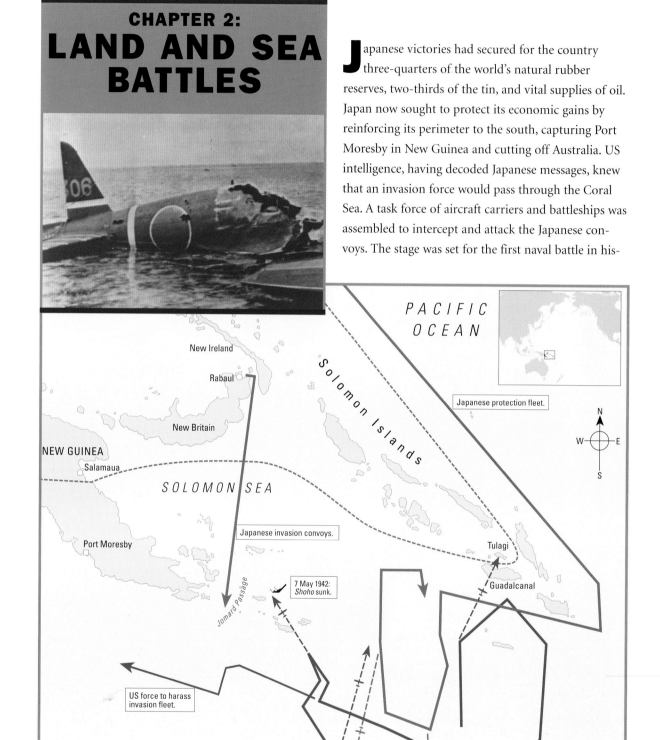

Japanese victories had secured for the country three-quarters of the world's natural rubber reserves, two-thirds of the tin, and vital supplies of oil. Japan now sought to protect its economic gains by reinforcing its perimeter to the south, capturing Port Moresby in New Guinea and cutting off Australia. US intelligence, having decoded Japanese messages, knew that an invasion force would pass through the Coral Sea. A task force of aircraft carriers and battleships was assembled to intercept and attack the Japanese convoys. The stage was set for the first naval battle in his-

PACIFIC OCEAN

New Ireland

Rabaul

Japanese protection fleet.

New Britain

Solomon Islands

NEW GUINEA

Salamaua

SOLOMON SEA

N
W — E
S

Port Moresby

Japanese invasion convoys.

Tulagi

Jomard Passage

7 May 1942:
Shoho sunk.

Guadalcanal

US force to harass invasion fleet.

CORAL SEA

Airgroup rendezvous with US fleet after Tulagi raid.

8 May 1942:
Lexington sunk.

	Japanese convoys and fleet
	US Fleet
	Japanese carrier-borne aircraft
	US carrier-borne aircraft
- - -	Extent of Japanese occupation

7 May 1942:
Sims sunk.

0   200 miles
0   200 kilometres

The battle of the Coral Sea was fought 4-8 May 1942 between US and Japanese navies.

tory in which the opposing sides never sighted one another, but relied on scout aircraft to direct attacks against one another's warships from the air.

The *Shokaku* and the *Zuikaku* were both Japanese carriers and, along with destroyers and cruisers, their job was to protect the invasion convoys aiming to land men at Port Moresby and Tulagi in the Solomon Islands. The convoys also had their own light carrier, the *Shoho*. On 5 May 1942, the US force assembled 650 km south of Guadalcanal. Two days earlier, Japanese ships landing at Tulagi had been attacked but the US plan now was to head for the Jomard Passage and to intercept the main Japanese invasion convoy.

BATTLE AT SEA

On 7 May 1942 US scout aircraft spotted the convoy, which then turned back to wait and see what would happen. The *Shoho* was attacked and sunk by aircraft from the USS *Lexington* and *Yorktown*. Japanese scout

planes, like the American ones earlier in the day, were unable to find the enemy aircraft carriers, but they did find and sink a destroyer, USS *Sims*.

On 8 May, both sides located one another and launched full air strikes from their carriers. While equal in numbers, the Japanese had the superior Mitsubishi A6M Zero fighter and the *Lexington* was sunk after being hit by bombs and torpedoes. The *Yorktown* was damaged. The *Shokaku* was also damaged but the *Zuikaku* was never located.

In one sense, the result of the haphazard battle of the Coral Sea was a draw; both sides suffered losses but neither side was dealt a knock-out blow. In the long run, however, the USA could be pleased with the result: the enemy's attempt to capture Port Morseby was blocked and, with one carrier sunk and another badly damaged, the Japanese were weakened in advance of the next and more decisive sea battle that was about to take place.

BATTLE OF THE CORAL SEA

US aircraft carriers	2	Lost	1
Japanese aircraft carriers	3	Lost	1
US cruisers	5	Lost	0
Japanese cruisers	6	Lost	0
US destroyers	9	Lost	1
Japanese destroyers	7	Lost	0

[From *The Second World War in the East*, H.P. Willmott]

Opposite page: A Japanese fighter shot down during the battle of the Coral Sea and (below) the *Shokaku* on fire and taking evasive action during the same battle.

WORLD WAR II: THE PACIFIC

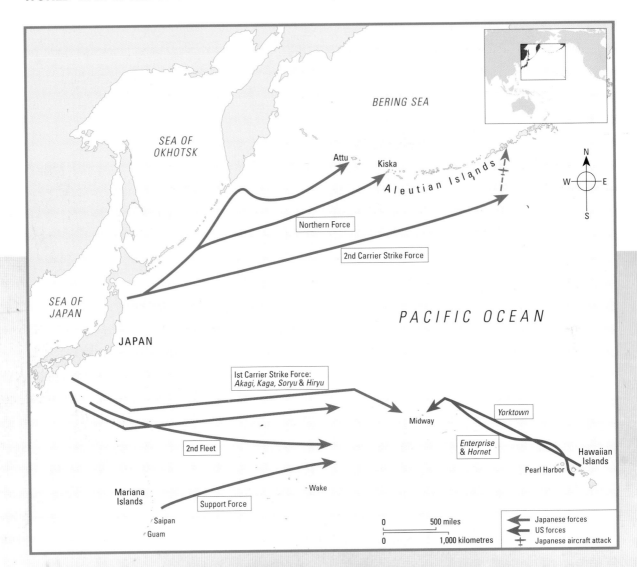

BERING SEA

SEA OF OKHOTSK

Attu

Kiska

Aleutian Islands

Northern Force

2nd Carrier Strike Force

SEA OF JAPAN

PACIFIC OCEAN

JAPAN

1st Carrier Strike Force:
Akagi, Kaga, Soryu & Hiryu

Yorktown

Midway

Enterprise & Hornet

Hawaiian Islands

Pearl Harbor

2nd Fleet

Mariana Islands

Wake

Support Force

Saipan

Guam

| 0 | 500 miles |
| 0 | 1,000 kilometres |

Japanese forces
US forces
Japanese aircraft attack

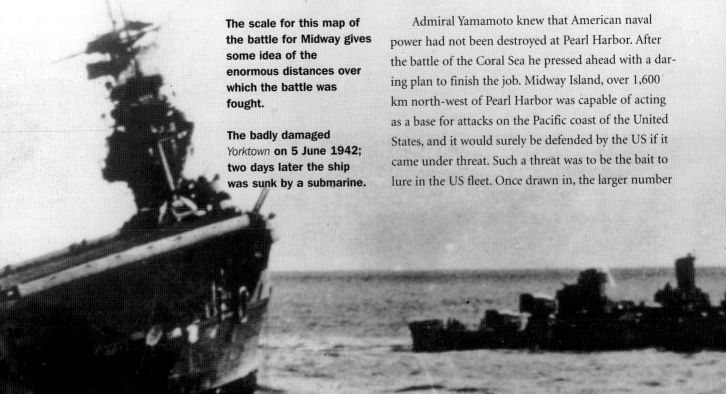

The scale for this map of the battle for Midway gives some idea of the enormous distances over which the battle was fought.

The badly damaged *Yorktown* on 5 June 1942; two days later the ship was sunk by a submarine.

Admiral Yamamoto knew that American naval power had not been destroyed at Pearl Harbor. After the battle of the Coral Sea he pressed ahead with a daring plan to finish the job. Midway Island, over 1,600 km north-west of Pearl Harbor was capable of acting as a base for attacks on the Pacific coast of the United States, and it would surely be defended by the US if it came under threat. Such a threat was to be the bait to lure in the US fleet. Once drawn in, the larger number of Japanese aircraft carriers, battleships and destroyers lying in wait could destroy the enemy fleet. The plan also called for a smaller attack on the Aleutian Islands, north of Midway, as a diversion to split the US fleet.

THE CODE HAD BEEN CRACKED

What Yamamoto did not know was that coded Japanese radio messages had been cracked, and Admiral Chester W. Nimitz, commander of the US Pacific Fleet, was aware of the plan. Early on 4 June 1942 Japanese carrier aircraft attacked Midway. Their carrier fleet was located by US aircraft from the *Yorktown* but their early attacks failed and thirty-five US planes were lost. Then US Admiral Raymond A. Spruance, with the *Enterprise* and *Hornet*, took the opportunity for a surprise attack. Three Japanese carriers were caught while they were refuelling after attacking Midway. A small group of American dive-bombers targeted the carriers. Their defenders were in disarray, and quickly the ships were turned into burning wrecks.

A fourth Japanese carrier, *Hiryu*, escaped and was able to join in an attack on the *Yorktown* on the afternoon of the same day. The *Yorktown* was seriously damaged, and would later be sunk by a Japanese submarine, but *Hiryu* was also damaged beyond repair. Spruance then chose to withdraw, which was just as well because there was another Japanese force advancing on Midway under Admiral Yamamoto.

The battle of Midway was the first decisive defeat in the Pacific of the Japanese. It signalled a shift in the balance of power in favour of the USA, although this was not recognized at the time. The Japanese lost four carriers, 225 aircraft and a cruiser; the Americans lost

A Farewell Drink

Japanese Admiral Kusaka recalled the last moments on board *Hiryu*: 'When it was ascertained that the ship was in a sinking condition, Admiral Yamaguchi and Captain Kaku decided that they would go down with the ship. They all shared some naval biscuits and drank a glass of water in a last ceremony. Admiral Yamaguchi gave his hat to one of his staff officers and asked him to give it to his family; then there was some joking among them – the captain and the admiral – that their duties were finished when the ship sank.'
[From *The Pacific Campaign*, Dan Van der Vat]

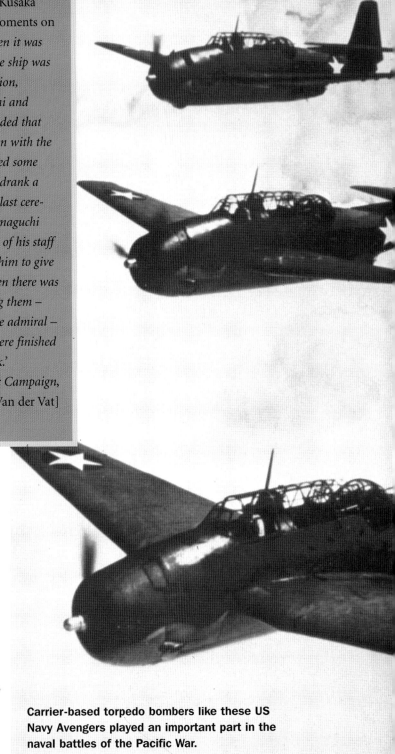

Carrier-based torpedo bombers like these US Navy Avengers played an important part in the naval battles of the Pacific War.

one carrier, 146 planes and a destroyer. Hundreds of lives were lost on both sides.

The Solomon Islands (see page 14) stretch for about 1,000 km across the south Pacific. The Japanese had a base there at Rabaul, and a smaller presence on Tulagi and Guadalcanal. After the battle of Midway, neither side had gained control of the south Pacific and so the island of Guadalcanal became a battleground for the continuing struggle between Japan and the USA.

The battle started on 7 August 1942 when 10,000 US troops landed on Guadalcanal. Then, unexpectedly, Japanese warships from Rabaul appeared nearby off Savo island and sank four cruisers sent there to protect the landings. Over 1,000 Allied seamen lost their lives in the Slot, in that part of the seaway between the Florida islands and Guadalcanal that

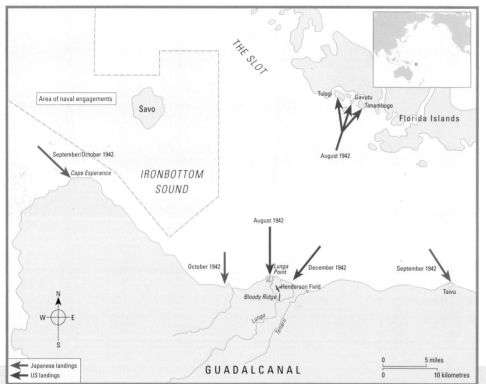

THE SLOT

Area of naval engagements

Savo

Tulagi
Gavutu
Tanambogo

Florida Islands

August 1942

September/October 1942

Cape Esperance

IRONBOTTOM SOUND

August 1942

October 1942

Lunga Point

December 1942

September 1942

Henderson Field

Taivu

Bloody Ridge

Lunga

Tenaru

N
W—E
S

Japanese landings
US landings

0   5 miles
0   10 kilometres

G U A D A L C A N A L

The land battle for Guadalcanal was mostly restricted to a relatively small area around Henderson Field airfield.

US Marines coming ashore from a landing craft to join the battle on Guadalcanal.

US Marines examine a Japanese machine-gun emplacement in the malaria-ridden jungle on the island of Guadalcanal.

became known as Ironbottom Sound because of all the ships that were sunk there. The Japanese then chose to withdraw rather than stay and attack the transport ships, to avoid the risk of counterattacks from the air.

THE BATTLE FOR GUADALCANAL

The island of New Guinea (see page 20) and its capital Port Moresby, to the north of Australia, also became part of the struggle for control of the south-west Pacific. The troops on Guadalcanal were left unprotected and undersupplied, but they did complete an airfield that was left unfinished by the Japanese on the north coast. Named Henderson Field, it became a target for the Japanese when they landed their own troops on the island. Between September and November, each side was reinforced with thousands more soldiers who fought one another desperately in a series of engagements, with Japanese troops advancing to within 900 metres of the airfield in the battle of Bloody Ridge in September.

The land battles were accompanied by a series of seven naval engagements. In November, a three-day sea battle unfolded as the Japanese attempted to land fresh troops while aircraft from Henderson Field attacked them. No single engagement proved conclusive over five months of fighting but the US forces gradually took control. By January 1943 they had some 50,000 troops on the island. Finally the remaining Japanese, more than 10,000 of them, were evacuated from the island at night without being spotted by their enemy.

With the battle for Guadalcanal, close-combat fighting in tropical jungle conditions become a feature of the Pacific war. The island, in its own right, was not worth the losses that both sides suffered, but in the

long run this was the first successful US land battle in the Pacific and it marked a turning point in the war. Australians became heavily involved in the fighting,

LOSSES AT GUADALCANAL

Naval engagements, 12-14 November 1942

US battleships	2	Lost 0
Japanese battleships	3	Lost 2
US heavy cruisers	2	Lost 0
Japanese heavy cruisers	2	Lost 0
US light cruisers	2	Lost 0
Japanese light cruisers	3	Lost 0
US destroyers	12	Lost 6
Japanese destroyers	19	Lost 3

Land engagements, August 1942-February 1943

US troops	60,000
Killed	1,600
Japanese troops	36,000
Killed/missing	15,000
Died of sickness	10,000

[From *The Second World War in the East*, H.P. Willmott]

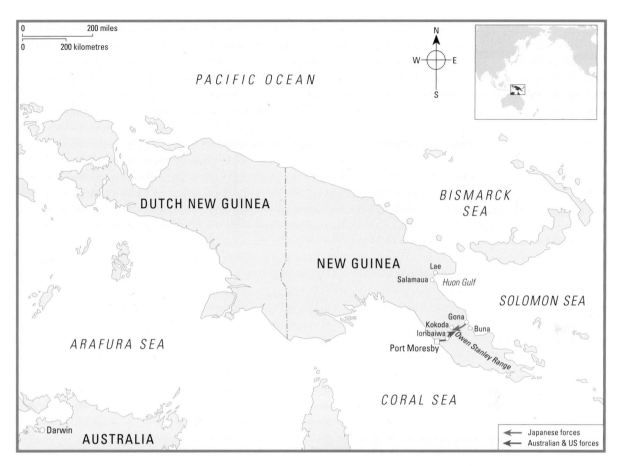

New Guinea was divided into a Dutch half, part of the Netherlands East Indies, and an Australian-controlled half.

not least because their own country was coming under threat. By October 1943, there were nearly half a million Australian infantry in the Pacific, under overall US control, compared with fewer than 200,000 US land troops.

Japanese forces had landed on the northern coast of New Guinea in March 1942. They intended to move overland and capture Port Moresby, but the battle of the Coral Sea interrupted this operation. After the battle of Midway, the US felt confident enough to try to clear this Japanese force. General MacArthur was in overall command as Australian troops moved north from Port Moresby to engage the enemy. Meanwhile, on 12 July 1942, more Japanese had landed on the northern coast and moved south. There was only one route across the 4,000-m high Owen Stanley mountains that divided Port Moresby from the north coast. It was an almost impassable mud track through jungle and over high ridges, known as the Kokoda trail. It became

General MacArthur passing Australian troops on their way to fight in the north of New Guinea.

a desperate battleground as Japanese and Australian soldiers fought one another and struggled to survive in the jungle. Soldiers who lost the trail died and many Japanese also starved to death because of inadequate supplies of food.

Fighting over the Kokoda trail lasted until the Japanese withdrew in September. Australians and US troops then attacked Gona and Buna but it was not until January 1943 that the area was cleared of

MARCHING IN THE JUNGLE

Ogawa Masatsugu, a Japanese soldier, remembers the campaign in New Guinea and the terrible conditions that drove many soldiers to suicide: *'It rained for more than half a year straight. Our guns rusted. Iron just rotted way. Wounds wouldn't heal … You slipped and fell, got up, went sprawling, stood up, like an army of marching mud dolls. It went on without end, just trudging through the muddy water, following the legs of someone in front of you … All battlefields are wretched places. New Guinea was ghastly. There was a saying during the war: "Burma is hell; from New Guinea no one returns alive."* *… In the army, anyone over thirty was an old man. Twenty-six or twenty-seven, that was your peak. The young soldiers, serving for the first time, didn't know how to pace themselves and died quickly, though there were many strong men, fishermen and farmers, among them.'*

[From *Japan At War*, Haruko Taya Cook and Theodore F. Cook]

The bodies of slain American soldiers lying on the beach at Buna on the north-east coast of New Guinea, January 1943.

Japanese. Meanwhile, from Lae and Salamaua on the north-west coast, another Japanese advance on Port Moresby got under way. By the end of February, it had been driven back. Japanese forces had been stretched in New Guinea because the battle for Guadalcanal was taking place at the same time.

CHAPTER 3:
THE VICTIMS

Chinese civilians flee for their lives during a Japanese bombing raid on Canton in 1938.

Japan's rapid victories in the first half of 1942 established a new empire that stretched for thousands of kilometres, from mainland China to far-flung Pacific islands. It affected the lives of millions of ordinary citizens. Japan proclaimed the creation of a *Greater East Asia Co-Prosperity Scheme* that would liberate Asians from white colonial rule. At first, many people in the occupied countries welcomed this idea and saw the Japanese as liberators. In Sumatra, local people rose in rebellion against their Dutch rulers and arrested those

The Japanese, having conquered a vast area, were faced with the problem of keeping it under their control during the Pacific War.

Territory controlled by the Japanese, 1942

who tried to flee before the Japanese arrived. Later, peasants were forced into slave labour by the Japanese and an estimated four million people died as a result of the Japanese occupation of the Netherlands East Indies (Indonesia).

While the Japanese were fighting in China, they suspected Chinese living overseas of supporting their enemy. In Singapore, many thousands of Chinese were driven to beaches and machine-gunned by Japanese soldiers. It was not only the Chinese who were harshly treated. An estimated 200,000 women, mostly Korean but also Filipinos and some Dutch, were drafted into camps where they became 'comfort women', forced to provide sex for Japanese soldiers.

Neither the Japanese nor the Allies respected the culture of Pacific islanders and the islanders suffered terribly as a result. New Guineans, for example, died in tens of thousands as their land was bombed. Many were forced to work and fight for the opposing armies, meaning they could end up killing one another. Their traditional way of life came under severe stress as they struggled to cope: 'All the clans … who were once brave, courageous, and strong seemed to become like babies in their first day out of their mother's wombs. The landings of the Japanese, gun noises, and the actual sight of the ships … They could not run … It was a unique disaster beyond any-body's memory', recorded a New Guinean man.

Japanese victories between December 1941 and April 1942 led to huge num-

NOWHERE TO RUN TO

Pacific islanders had no choice but to endure the battles that erupted on their islands. One man describes how they tried to survive: *'All of us were in holes … We were hungry and thirsty, but no one could go out. If you travelled outside you would disappear … Then in their coming the [American] warriors were not straight in their working. They came to the shelter of ours, guns ready, and looked toward us inside. So great was our fear that we were all in a corner, like kittens. And then they yelled and threw in a hand grenade … When it burst, the whole shelter was torn apart … Earth fragments struck us, but the others in the other half, they died.'*
[From *The Second World War: A People's History*, Joanna Bourke]

Pacific islanders, like these on Guadalcanal helping US troops to build an airfield runway, became involved in the conflict in various ways.

The course of the Burma-Siam [Thailand] railway. It was built so that the Japanese did not have to send supplies to Burma by sea routes that would expose them to enemy attacks.

Allied prisoners-of-war awaiting internment after surrendering in the Philippines.

bers of soldiers and European civilians being taken prisoner. Around 70,000 troops surrendered in Singapore, plus 10,000 US soldiers and 62,000 Filipinos on the Bataan peninsula. There were a quarter of a million Dutch nationals in the Netherlands East Indies, 3,000 British in Hong Kong, 4,500 in Singapore, including about 300 children. Most of these people were interned and many did not survive the harsh conditions, poor diet and lack of medical facilities in the prison camps.

FORCED INTO SLAVE LABOUR

Food rations for prisoners kept them barely alive and they were forced to work on railway lines, coal mines, roads, docks and factories. Millions of peasants were forced into slave labour on Java, and in Siam the Japanese used prisoners of war (POWs) and civilians to dig a railway line to Burma through 420 km of mountainous jungle. Around 300,000 Asians from Malaya, Burma and the Netherlands East Indies were persuaded to work on the railway line, having no idea of the starvation diet and brutal conditions awaiting them. In addition, 60,000 Australian, British and Dutch POWs were transported to Siam to work on the railway. Conditions were awful for everyone, but

Many POWs in Japanese camps, kept alive with the barest minimum of food but still expected to work hard, never survived their ordeal.

Asians, very many of whom were women and children, suffered the worst. As many as one in three died; among the Allied prisoners of war, one in five died. Dr Hardie, a POW working on the Burma-Siam railway, kept a secret diary in which he recorded the plight of Asian prisoners: 'People who have been near these camps speak with bated breath of the state of affairs – corpses rotting unburied in the jungle, almost complete lack of sanitation, a frightful stench, overcrowding, swarms of flies.'

The Pacific War was an especially vicious conflict and part of the reason for this lies in a deep-rooted racism and nastionalism that marked the attitudes of the countries fighting one another.

BATAAN DEATH MARCH

William Dyess survived the death march but well understood what could have happened to him:

'Their ferocity grew as we marched on into the afternoon … I stumbled over a man writhing in the hot dust of the road. He was a Filipino soldier who had been bayoneted through his stomach. Within a quarter of a mile I walked past another. This soldier prisoner had been rolled into the path of the trucks and crushed beneath the heavy wheels.

The huddled and smashed figures beside the road eventually became commonplace to us. The human mind has an amazing faculty of adjusting to shock.'

[From How It Happened: World War II, edited by Jon E. Lewis]

The Japanese saw the US and Europe as wanting to make colonies out of the whole of Asia. They were seen as enemies in racial terms, hypocrites who would not admit to their own greed in wanting to control Asia. Racial attitudes took hold as Japan's own ambitions in Asia were blocked by the US. The views of military leaders who accused the United States and Britain of imperialism and of wanting to humiliate the Japanese race by not accepting them as equals gained influence in Japan.

Allied prisoners-of-war during the Bataan Death March; of those who survived the march, another 16,000 died in the first few weeks at their destination camp.

RACISM AND THE BRUTALITY OF WAR
The Japanese military code of conduct did not accept that a soldier could surrender honourably. Japanese soldiers were encouraged to think of themselves as noble warriors fighting a corrupt enemy, and an enemy who surrendered was next to worthless. Evidence of this brutal attitude came after the surrender of US and Philippine forces on the Bataan peninsula in 1942. Forced to march 105 km to a prison camp, the prisoners were clubbed and bayoneted along the way. Five to ten thousand Filipinos and over 600 Americans died on the trek, many from exhaustion and starvation.

The US forces and the Europeans and Australians had their own sense of

racial superiority. The commander of British forces in south-east Asia, Air Chief Marshal Sir Robert Brooke-Popham, described how in 1940: 'I had a good close-up, across the barbed wire, of various sub-human specimens dressed in dirty grey uniform, which I was informed were Japanese soldiers.' An American general congratulated his troops on the capture of an island by speaking of: 'The sincere admiration of the entire Third Fleet is yours for the hill-blasting, cave-smashing extermination of 11,000 slant-eyed gophers.'

Many of the soldiers fighting in the Pacific War had no previous experience of battle. They were young men who had been conscripted or volunteered for service, and the reality of combat was a terrible experience. The death of friends and fellow soldiers was

A Japanese soldier, bayonet at the ready, guards Allied prisoners during their forced march up the Bataan peninsula.

The course of the Death March up the Bataan peninsula to the former Philippine Army Camp O'Donnell, over a hundred kilometres to the north.

awful and it hardened attitudes towards the enemy. One American soldier, George Peto, remembered how, after the death of a friend, 'that sure put a different perspective on my part in the war'. Peto went on to say how it changed and hardened his attitude towards the enemy and, in a similar kind of way, after the surrender on the Bataan peninsula, one group of prisoners were told by a Japanese officer how 'we're going to kill you because you killed many of our soldiers.' For soldiers on both sides, the war became personal.

Atrocities against soldiers and civilians were committed by both sides. It was not unusual for captured

'A KILLING MACHINE'

Nelson Perry, an American soldier, remembers how the Pacific war turned ordinary individuals into something else: *'Men in combat … cease being individuals; they become part of a machine that kills and that bayonets people, that sets fire to people, that laughs at people when they're running down the trail screaming in agony and you laugh at them. It's because you're no longer an individual, you're part of a machine, a killing machine.'*

Yamauchi Taeko, who surrendered on Saipan, made a similar observation: *'The American soldiers had been demons on the battlefield, ready to kill me in an instant. Now here they were, right in front of my eyes. Relaxed. Sprawled on top of jeeps, shouting, "Hey!" Joking with each other.'*

[From *Hell in the Pacific*, Jonathan Lewis and Ben Steele, and *Japan At War*, Haruko Taya Cook and Theodore F. Cook]

An American medic on Saipan; wounded soldiers were evacuated to hospital ships waiting offshore.

US soldiers remember and mourn their fallen comrades on Saipan.

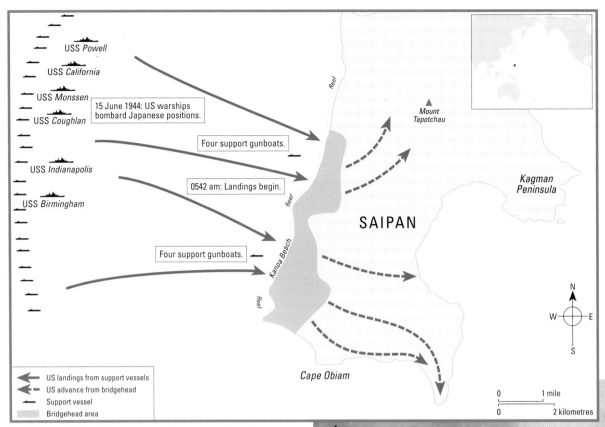

USS *Powell*
USS *California*
USS *Monssen*
USS *Coughlan*
USS *Indianapolis*
USS *Birmingham*

15 June 1944: US warships bombard Japanese positions.

Four support gunboats.

0542 am: Landings begin.

Four support gunboats.

Reef

Mount Tapotchau

Kagman Peninsula

SAIPAN

Kanoa Beach

Reef

Cape Obiam

N
W — E
S

US landings from support vessels
US advance from bridgehead
Support vessel
Bridgehead area

0 — 1 mile
0 — 2 kilometres

Japanese resistance on Saipan was fierce, despite intense bombardment by US battleships for two days before the landings.

Determined Japanese forces dug out defensive positions on Saipan which had to be destroyed one by one by US troops.

soldiers to be killed rather than taken prisoner. The capture of the Japanese-controlled island of Saipan in the Marianas involved ferocious fighting that illustrates just how vicious the Pacific war became. American troops landed on the island, 22 km long, in mid-June 1944. Three days had been planned for the island's capture but fierce Japanese resistance stretched this into three weeks. Some 4,000 Americans were killed or injured on the beaches in the first two days. The Japanese then withdrew to a rocky area around Mount Tapotchau.

One night early in July a desperate all-out attack, known as a banzai, was launched by Japanese infantry troops. Advancing in one massed group, regardless of the enemy's answering fire, the banzai turned into a suicidal attack. As many as 4,000 Japanese may have

lost their lives in this one action. A few days later, in a state of mass hysteria, thousands of Japanese civilians living on the island jumped off the cliffs in defiance of American victory. Nearly 8,000 civilians died on Saipan, bringing total Japanese losses to over 30,000; American losses were 3,426 dead.

CHAPTER 4:
FIGHTING BACK

Raising the flag on one of the Solomon Islands, symbolizing the successful expulsion of Japanese forces by US troops.

Early in 1943, with Guadalcanal captured and the enemy being forced off New Guinea, the Americans felt confident enough to push forward with their plan to capture the main Japanese base at Rabaul on New Britain. Troops landed on New Georgia at the end of June, but it was 5 August before the island's airfield was captured. There were battles at sea as well as fierce fighting on land that took their toll of inexperienced American troops who were not battle-hardened.

By the middle of August, flights from New Georgia's airfield supported new landings on the neighbouring island of Vella Lavella. Over a thousand Americans lost their lives taking the two islands and more than twice that number of Japanese died on New Georgia alone. By November, troops had landed on Bougainville and the following month saw landings on the Green Islands. Rabaul, however, was heavily defended by soldiers living in specially built tunnels. A land attack was put off and the island of New Britain was bombed heavily from the air until the Japanese garrison was put out of action.

Both the US Army under General MacArthur and the US Navy under Admiral Nimitz were in action against the Japanese. There was a certain amount of rivalry between the two forces, but it never became a

An assault boat carrying US Marines to land at Empress Augusta Bay on 1 November 1943, at the start of a hard-fought campaign to clear Bougainville island of its Japanese garrison.

The map shows the main theatres of war as US and Japanese forces wrestled for control of the Solomons.

PACIFIC OCEAN

Rabaul
Green Islands
New Britain
Bougainville
Solomon Islands
Choiseul
SOLOMON SEA
Vella Lavella
New Georgia
NEW GUINEA
Russell Island
Henderson Field
Guadalcanal
CORAL SEA

0   200 miles
0   250 kilometres

N W E S

US offensive

US troops observe the bodies of Japanese soldiers killed on a Guadalcanal beach after an unsuccessful attempt to land reinforcements.

serious problem. Both commanders were helped by the fact that by the end of 1943 the American war economy had new aircraft, tanks and ships rolling off the production lines in record time. By early 1944, a new aircraft was being produced every 294 seconds. Also, American submarines, sailing from Pearl Harbor and Australian bases, achieved more and more success

TORMENTS OF WAR

Ogawa Tamotsu, a Japanese medic, was ordered to kill patients who were too ill to care for:

'I was at the front almost six years, in China, and then in the South Pacific. The final year was the most horrible. It was just a hell. I was a medic in a field hospital on New Britain Island ... We were five or six medics with one to two hundred patients to care for ... In the beginning it was hard to do it, then I got used to it and didn't cry any more. I became a murderer ... Sometimes, when I look back, I even get a sense of fulfilment that I survived. Sometimes, though, it's all nothingness. I think to myself: I deserve a death sentence. I didn't kill just one or two. Only war allows this – these torments I have to bear until I die. My war will continue until that moment.'

[From *Japan at War*, Haruko Taya Cook and Theodore F. Cook]

An American Marine hurls a grenade at an enemy machine-gun post during the grim battle for Tarawa in November 1943.

against enemy shipping. The Japanese found it difficult to maintain supply lines and this seriously weakened their ability to keep fighting the war.

A KILLING ZONE
The south-to-north advance on Japan, through New Guinea and eventually the Philippines, was under the command of General MacArthur. Admiral Nimitz preferred an 'island hop-ping' strategy, starting in the central Pacific and con-tinuing through the Caroline Islands and the Marianas, before pushing close to Japan through Iwo Jima and Okinawa. After the decision to bypass Rabaul in the south-west, the initiative shifted to the central Pacific. Nimitz's campaign began with the tiny island of Tarawa.

Triangular in shape and nowhere rising more than 3.5 m above sea level, Tarawa is one of sixteen atolls forming the Gilbert Islands. It is made up of forty-seven coral islands, the largest of which, Betio, is only 4 km long. It was invaded in November 1943. The landing area, divided into zones called Red 1, 2 and 3 by the US, was expertly protected by nearly 5,000 elite troops under Japanese Rear-Admiral Shibasaki. A three-metre high barricade of coconut logs with steel clamps was constructed off the shoreline to channel the invaders into a killing zone. Here, they faced heavy gunfire from emplacements dug in behind timber and sand defences, while others were protected behind con-crete. Tons of shells were fired at the island's defences but they had little effect, and the Japanese were able to

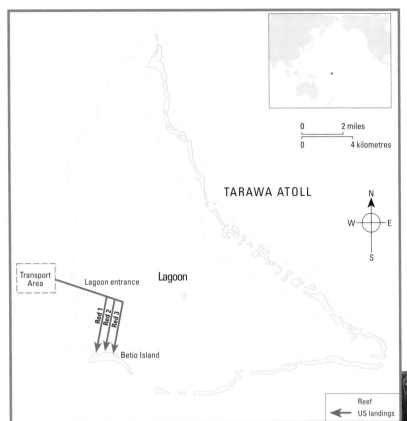

TARAWA ATOLL

0 2 miles
0 4 kilometres

N
W — E
S

Transport Area

Lagoon entrance

Lagoon

Red 1
Red 2
Red 3

Betio Island

Reef
US landings

but by the end of the third day the island was taken. Casualty figures released by the US Army indicated that only 17 Japanese prisoners, out of a garrison force of 4,836, survived. American dead numbered over 800, with more than 2,000 injured.

US troops and Japanese fought bitterly for possession of the coral island of Betio, part of Tarawa atoll. It is no larger than New York's Central Park.

US forces advancing in Tarawa, one of the most heavily fortified islands fought over during the Pacific War.

It was not until the second day, when American troops occupied part of the south shore and an area in the west, that reinforcements were able to land there. The Japanese eventually withdrew to the eastern end of the island and counterattacked with banzai charges,

'OUR ONLY ARMOUR WAS THE SHIRT ON OUR BACKS'

Bob Libby should have landed on Red 1 but his launch hit the coral reef and he leaped overboard:
'*The sound of screaming shells passed overhead, the unmistakeable crack of rifle fire zipped around our ears, heavy explosions on shore … the screams of the wounded were lost in this cacophony of sound – all the while we who survived so far still made our way to the beach to find some haven of safety, if such existed. … Every step of the way was a life and death situation; how anyone ever reached the shore is still mysterious to me as the enemy fire seemed to cover every inch between the reef and shore – there was no hiding place, no protection, our only armour was the shirt on our backs*'.

[From *Tarawa – A Hell of a Way to Die*, Derrick Wright]

After Tarawa, the next objective was a group of thirty-six central Pacific atolls called the Marshall Islands. US intelligence had decoded messages that indicated the Japanese expected an attack on the outer atolls. These atolls was weakened by bombing attacks from Tarawa but they were bypassed, not surrendering until the end of the war. US troops landed on Majura atoll on 30 January 1944 – the first US occupation of pre-war Japanese land – and in mid-February the more heavily defended Eniwetok was successfully attacked from the air and by land. In February the navy attacked the Japanese base of Truk, one of the Caroline Islands, dropping thirty times as much explosives as the Japanese had dropped on Pearl Harbor.

General MacArthur, not to be outdone by Admiral Nimitz, captured the Admiralty Islands in the south-

After capturing the Marshall and Caroline Islands, the Mariana Islands were the next obvious target.

A large transport vessel lands US troops in the Marshall Islands in April 1944.

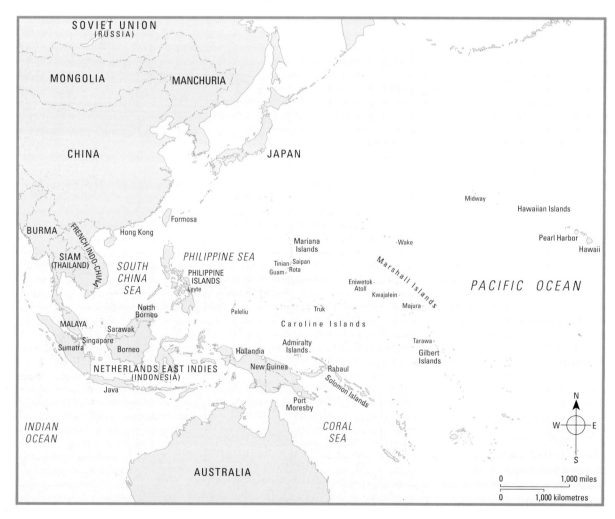

west and then seized Hollandia. The decoding of enemy messages allowed his forces also to leap over pockets of Japanese resistance, bypassing them and leaving them ineffective.

THE CENTRAL PACIFIC

In the central Pacific, the way was open for an attack on the Mariana Islands: Saipan, Tinian, Rota and Guam being the main targets. Launching invasions in February 1944, Guam was the last of the islands to be taken in August. The Japanese mounted a strike force of nine aircraft carriers to repel the invaders in what became the battle of the Philippine Sea in June. It was the biggest carrier battle of the war. The Japanese were the first to locate their enemy but their pilots were outnumbered and out-matched by US fighters. The next day, the Japanese fleet was located; one carrier was sunk and three damaged; American submarines had already sunk two others.

After the capture of the Mariana Islands, there was a decision to be made: whether to move closer to Japan via Formosa, or take back the Philippines. MacArthur and Nimitz agreed on the Philippines and planned to seize the Japanese-occupied coral island of Peleliu as protection for land-ings on Leyte in the Philippines. The capture of Peleliu turned into one of the war's bloodiest engagements, starting on 15 September and not ending until the end of November.

The Japanese knew that it was important to try to prevent the capture of the Philippines

US soldiers celebrate the capture of Eniwetok atoll in the Marshall Islands, a useful staging post which brought American aircraft within range of the Caroline Islands.

THE FORGOTTEN BATTLE

Equal in ferocity to the battle for Tarawa, the struggle for Peleliu received far less publicity during the war. Regarded as the Pacific War's 'forgotten battle', it is debatable whether it should ever have been fought because it made little difference to the capture of the Philippines. The human cost was terrible:

US

1,050 killed in action

150 died of wounds

5,450 wounded

36 missing

Japanese

10,900 killed

202 prisoners; 19 of which were Japanese, the rest being non-Japanese labourers

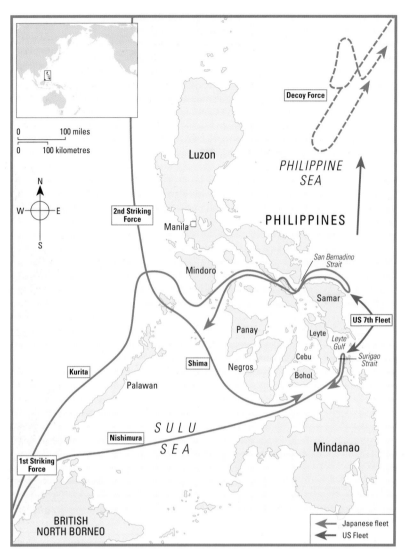

The Japanese 1st Striking Force split, with Nishimura heading east towards Leyte, and Kurita heading north-east.

Admiral Jizaburo Ozawa (1886-1963) played a successful part in the Leyte Gulf battle.

and so halt the US advance towards their home country. The plan was that Vice-Admiral Jizaburo Ozawa, in overall command of the operation, would divert the main US force by sailing four almost empty aircraft carriers to the north-east of the Philippines. The bulk of the Japanese naval force – comprising most of the warships Japan still had afloat – would be split between Vice-Admirals Kiyohide Shima and Takeo Kurita. Shima, aided by some of Kurita's ships under the command of Vice-Admiral Shoji Nishimura, would occupy Surigao Strait while Kurita would head for the San Bernardino Strait to the north. The American landing force would be caught in a pincer movement between

the two of them and wiped out along with their support ships.

THE BATTLE OF LEYTE GULF

The plan failed, partly because Nishimura's force was virtually destroyed by American battleships and cruisers and Shima, who was following behind, withdrew without joining the fight. The other, stronger force, under Kurita, was met the following morning, and the ensuing battle was a close-run affair. For the first time, kamikaze pilots, suicidally crashing their aircraft on to their targets, sunk an American ship. The outcome of the battle seemed to be in doubt when Kurita withdrew, to the surprise and relief of the Americans.

Choosing to engage the enemy in the battle of Leyte Gulf, the largest naval battle in world history, was a worthwhile gamble for the Japanese. Without the Philippines, they would be cut off from their fuel supplies in the Netherlands East Indies. The gamble failed. The Japanese lost most of the major naval ships that they possessed and ten thousand Japanese lost their

Japanese kamikaze pilots preparing for their suicide attacks on US warships.

BATTLE OF LEYTE GULF 24-5 OCTOBER 1944		
US: Fleet carriers	9	Lost 0
Japanese: Fleet carriers	1	Lost 1
US: Light carriers	8	Lost 1
Japanese: Light carriers	3	Lost 3
US: Escort carriers	29	Lost 2
Japanese: Escort carriers	0	
US: Battleships	12	Lost 0
Japanese: Battleships	9	Lost 3
US: Heavy cruisers	5	Lost 0
Japanese: Heavy cruisers	15	Lost 6
US: Light cruisers	20	Lost 0
Japanese: Light cruisers	5	Lost 4
US: Destroyers	162	Lost 4
Japanese: Destroyers	35	Lost 4

[From *The Second World War in the East*, H.P. Willmott]

lives, as well as 1,500 US servicemen. Historians have credited the Japanese with a superior strategy and criticized Admiral William Halsey, in charge of the US forces, for falling for Ozawa's decoy and failing to prevent Kurita from reaching Leyte Gulf.

The US victory allowed MacArthur to land thousands of troops on Leyte and by the end of the year the general was ready to return to Manila, the capital city of the Philippines.

General Tomoyuki Yamashita, commander of Japanese forces in the Philippines, did not plan to fight in Manila. He left about 20,000 troops in the city, under Rear-Admiral Iwabuchi, and withdrew northwards to harass the enemy. He even planned to grow

WORLD WAR II: THE PACIFIC

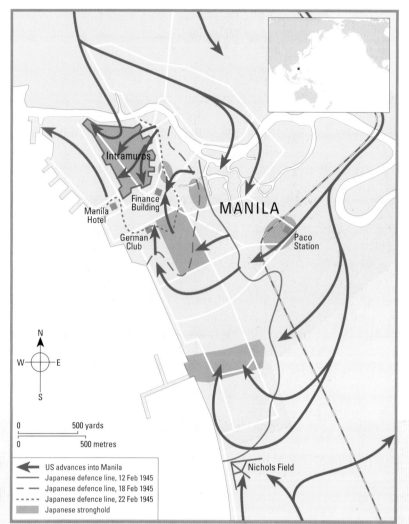

Intramuros

Manila
Hotel

Finance
Building

German
Club

MANILA

Paco
Station

N
W — E
S

```
0        500 yards
0        500 metres
```

US advances into Manila
Japanese defence line, 12 Feb 1945
Japanese defence line, 18 Feb 1945
Japanese defence line, 22 Feb 1945
Japanese stronghold

Nichols Field

his own crops in the north of Luzon (see page 36) to feed his troops. Iwabuchi, however, chose to avenge his country's disastrous naval defeats by fighting to the bitter end in the city. The resulting battle was the Pacific War's only battle in which Americans and Japanese fought in a city.

The first US advance from the south was stopped at Nichols Field and suffered 900 casualties. An advance from the north turned into a grim battle around Paco station where 300 Japanese held out for two days at a cost of 335 American casualties. On 15 February, Iwabuchi rejected Yamashita's order to break out of the city and made his last stand in Intramuros, a square mile of stone-built buildings surrounded by a high wall.

For every soldier killed in the battle for Manila, which had a population of 800,000, six civilians lost their lives.

An historic moment: General Douglas MacArthur returning to the Philippines, wading ashore on Leyte on 25 October 1944.

The corpse of an American soldier is carried on a stretcher through the ruins of Manila.

The Americans decided to employ heavy artillery and most of the city was reduced to rubble. Around 100,000 Filipino residents of the city lost their lives amidst the fighting, fires and explosions. The Japanese, knowing they were to die, took to slaughtering civilians, especially European residents. They attacked the German Club, where 1,500 European refugees were sheltering, killing hundreds with bayonets and clubs.

THE BATTLE FOR MANILA WAS

OVER In and around Intramuros, buildings were attacked and destroyed one by one. On 21 February the Manila Hotel was destroyed and four days later, with shells hitting his headquarters, Iwabuchi and others committed suicide. The last building in Japanese hands, the Finance Building, was reduced to rubble on 3 March. The battle for Manila was over.

The US, who lost 1,100 men, counted over 16,000 Japanese bodies. MacArthur, who knew he had nothing to be proud of, ordered that no public monuments commemorating the 'liberation' of the city should be erected in either the Philippines or the United States.

WAR TALK

'*We are very glad and grateful for the opportunity of being able to serve our country in this epic battle. Now, with what strength remains, we will daringly engage this enemy. Banzai to the Emperor! We are determined to fight to the last man*' Vice-Admiral Iwabuchi, 15 February 1945.

'*People of the Philippines: I have returned. By the grace of Almighty God our forces stand again on Philippine soil – soil consecrated in the blood of our two people ... Rally to me.*' General MacArthur, returning to the Philippines two and a half years after he had been forced to leave Corregidor.

[From *Atlas of World War II Battle Plans*, edited by S. Badsey, and *How It Happened: World War II*, edited by Jon E. Lewis]

CHAPTER 5:
CLOSING IN

A moment in time: US Marines attack a Japanese position on Iwo Jima, 23 March 1945.

to make it the most heavily fortified island that the Americans had yet attempted to capture. Mount Suribachi, an extinct volcano at the southern tip of the island, provided cover for defenders firing on the beach. Out of twenty-four US battalion commanders that came ashore in the first landing, nineteen were killed or wounded. Also, the volcanic ash on the beaches could be mixed with cement to make a hard concrete and the defenders used this to reinforce their positions across the island. The Marines fought hard to take the island – their courage symbolized by the famous photograph taken on 23 February of the Stars and Stripes being raised on Mount Suribachi.

The human cost of fighting for an island only eight kilometres long was appalling: over one in three of the US Marines, nearly 4,000 men, were killed; over 20,000 Japanese died. The casualty rate reached 75 per

The 'island hopping' strategy of the Americans had proved remarkably successful and the final objectives in the advance towards Japan were the two islands of Iwo Jima and Okinawa. There were three airfields on Iwo Jima, 1,050 km south of Tokyo, which could be used to provide fighter cover for long-range B-29 bombers attacking Japan from the Mariana Islands.

Beginning in February 1945, 110,000 US soldiers were put ashore on Iwo Jima and some 800 warships were involved in an operation that lasted well over a month. The island's first airfield was taken within forty-eight hours and the second within a week but the Japanese were securely positioned in the north of the island and it was here that the fiercest fighting unfolded.

The geography of Iwo Jima, one of the Volcano Islands, helped

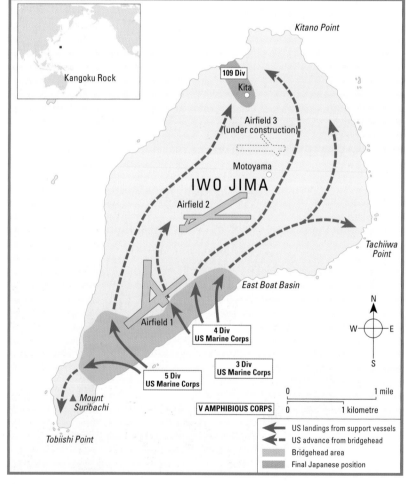

The Japanese dug in for stubborn resistance against US advances in the north of Iwo Jima.

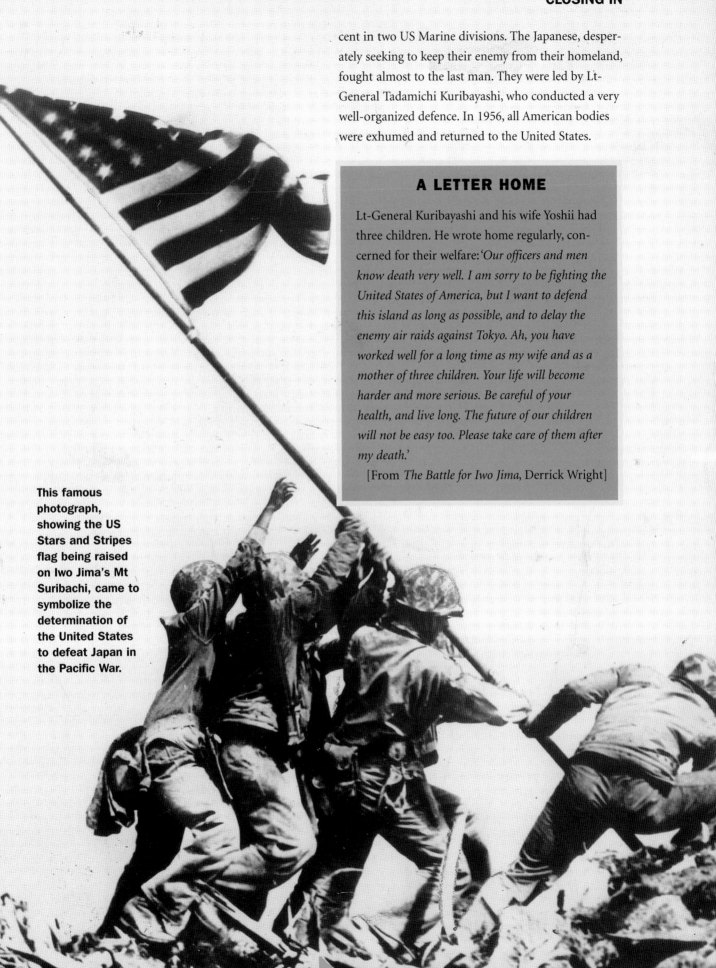

cent in two US Marine divisions. The Japanese, desperately seeking to keep their enemy from their homeland, fought almost to the last man. They were led by Lt-General Tadamichi Kuribayashi, who conducted a very well-organized defence. In 1956, all American bodies were exhumed and returned to the United States.

A LETTER HOME

Lt-General Kuribayashi and his wife Yoshii had three children. He wrote home regularly, concerned for their welfare: *'Our officers and men know death very well. I am sorry to be fighting the United States of America, but I want to defend this island as long as possible, and to delay the enemy air raids against Tokyo. Ah, you have worked well for a long time as my wife and as a mother of three children. Your life will become harder and more serious. Be careful of your health, and live long. The future of our children will not be easy too. Please take care of them after my death.'*

[From *The Battle for Iwo Jima*, Derrick Wright]

This famous photograph, showing the US Stars and Stripes flag being raised on Iwo Jima's Mt Suribachi, came to symbolize the determination of the United States to defeat Japan in the Pacific War.

Fifty years after the battle, Japanese volunteers were still returning to Iwo Jima to look for the remains of missing soldiers to cremate and return the ashes to Japan.

The island of Okinawa was the final stepping-stone to Japan. The island, 96 km long, had safe harbours from which an invasion of Japan could be launched, as well as airfields. It was vital for the Japanese to defend it and the United States, aware of this, mounted the most complex operation in the Pacific War to secure its capture. The huge scale of the resources employed gives a good idea of just how inevitable it was that Japan would lose the war. More oil and petrol was supplied to the naval forces between March and June 1945 than Japan imported in the whole of 1944. Over half a million troops were involved and more than 1,200 warships. Over 90,000

A SOLDIER'S NIGHTMARE

In 1984, John Garcia recalled Okinawa. The Japanese woman he refers to was someone he shot in error, mistaking her for a soldier: '*I had friends who were Japanese and I kept thinking every time I pulled a trigger on a man or pushed a flamethrower down into a hole: What is this person's family gonna say when he doesn't come back? He's got a wife, he's got children, somebody ... I'd get up each day and start drinking. How else could I fight the war? Sometimes we made the booze, sometimes we bought it from the navy...*
Oh, I still lose nights of sleep because of that woman I shot. I still lose a lot of sleep. I still dream about her. I dreamed about it perhaps two weeks ago.'
[From '*The Good War': An Oral History of World War II*, edited by Studs Terkel]

A wounded Japanese officer emerges from a cave and surrenders on Okinawa.

American shipping in waves of massed attacks called *kikusui* (floating chrysanthemums). They inflicted huge damage but, in a struggle between seamen fighting to live and pilots dying in order to fight, the island's capture could not be prevented.

ON OKINAWA   On Okinawa itself, it took three weeks to conquer the Motubo peninsula where Japanese defenders were concentrated. The other main area of fighting was south of a line between Naha and Yonabaru and it was 27 May before Naha was in US hands. Out of a garrison force of nearly 80,000 men, only 7,400 Japanese were taken prisoner. Over 7,500 soldiers died and nearly 5,000 seamen lost their lives on the US side.

The near-suicidal resistance of the Japanese to US advances made the idea of invading Japan itself a fearsome prospect. This led to a new policy of bombing Japanese cities, put into effect from March 1945 until the end of the war.

Major-General Curtis E. LeMay, in charge of the

missions were flown by carrier-based US aircraft in the course of the campaign and the carrier force remained at sea for a continuous period of three months. It has been calculated that one of the American divisions landed with enough food to supply the city of Colombus, Ohio, for a month.

The Japanese knew they could not win. The giant *Yamato* battleship and eight destroyers left Japan to join the battle with only enough fuel for a one-way voyage. Nearly 2,000 kamikaze missions attacked

Marines of the US 6th Division take cover during the advance on Naha, the capital of Okinawa, where Japanese forces were concentrated.

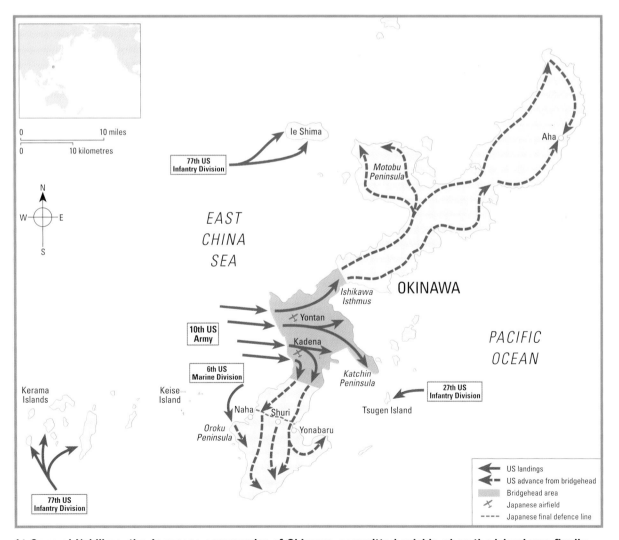

Lt-General Ushijima, the Japanese commander of Okinawa, committed suicide when the island was finally taken by US forces.

The bombardment of Japan was carried out by almost 600 bombers which eventually could attack almost any target they chose, encountering little resistance. The destruction was immense.

bombardment, began by abandoning the earlier policy of daytime, high-altitude raids that were meant to hit particular targets. This was not proving effective and the new policy involved night raids flying at far lower altitudes. Areas of cities were now subjected to bombing that caused fires rather than explosions. Densely packed Japanese cities had many wooden buildings and fires spread rapidly. All Japanese cities became targets and around ten million people were killed, injured or made homeless as a result.

Tokyo, the capital city, suffered especially from firestorms caused by intense bombing. Fires consumed more and more oxygen, turning the city into one large inferno, with temperatures rising to 800°C, fanned by hurricane force winds. In one raid on 9 March, 83,000 civilians died.

REDUCED TO RUINS Between mid-May and mid-June, six of Japan's major industrial cities were largely reduced to ruins by B-29 bombers. These huge aircraft also bombed during the day, protected by fighters from Iwo Jima. They shot down so many

Loading bombs onto one of the 3,970 B-29 Superfortress bombers built by the US for use only in the Pacific War. The aircraft was based on Saipan Island, in the Mariana Islands.

Japanese fighters trying to hit the B-29s that the Japanese grounded their remaining aircraft, keeping them for use against the expected land invasion. By August, Japan's economy had been largely disabled as a result of the bombing raids and over a quarter of a million civilians had been killed. Most Japanese now realized that their country could not win the war, although military leaders insisted that further resistance would force the United States to negotiate a peace that was not too unfavourable for Japan.

'BLOWN AWAY'

Schoolgirl Funato Kazuyo, with her two brothers, Kōichi and Minoru, and her younger sister, Hiroko, were in a shelter [in Tokyo] when they realized a fire was heading towards them: *'When we went out, we could see to the west, in the direction of Fukagawa, everything was bright red. The north wind was incredibly strong. The drone of the planes was an overwhelming roar, shaking earth and sky. Everywhere, incendiary bombs were falling* … [They ran from the fire and took shelter elsewhere] *'We lay flat on our stomachs, thinking we would be all right if the fire was gone by morning, but the fire kept pelting down on us. Minoru suddenly let out a horrible scream and leapt out of the shelter, flames shooting out of his back. Kōichi stood up calling, "Minoru!" and instantly, he too, was blown away. Only Hiroko and I remained.'*

[From *Japan At War*, Haruko Taya Cook and Theodore F. Cook]

Nearly half the entire urban area of Tokyo was flattened by US bombing raids between March and June 1945.

World War II was drawing to a close. A defeated Nazi Germany had surrendered to the Allies in May 1945 and the US advance towards Japan was reaching a climax. Meanwhile, war was still raging in another, less well-known theatre in China and Burma.

CHIANG KAI-SHEK

Chinese nationalists under Chiang Kai-shek, who had been fighting Japanese forces since the invasion in 1937, were supported by the Allies and supplied with arms and money. The Japanese invasion of Burma early in 1942 cut off the supply line to the nationalists and fighting developed for the control of Burma. The turning point in this war came in March 1944 when Allied troops, mostly Indians under the British General William Slim, were attacked by the Japanese at Imphal in India. The opposing armies battled it out for months but the Japanese were gradually worn down and by July they were forced to withdraw. General Slim pushed into Burma and captured Mandalay and then the capital, Rangoon.

The success of the US 'island hopping' strategy then made the fate of Burma less important to the Allies. Another reason was the realization that Chiang Kai-shek was not an effective ally. It was his communist rival, Mao Tsetung, who was more useful in helping to tie up about a million Japanese troops in China.

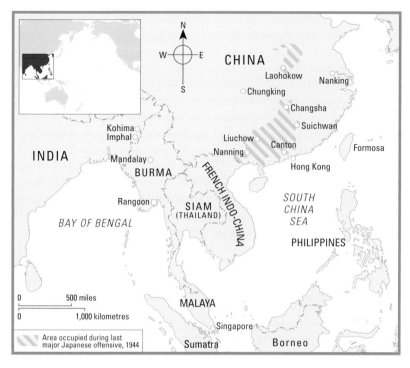

Fighting in China tied down around a million Japanese soldiers and saw Mao Tse-tung and his Communist army emerge as the future face of the country. The map shows the area occupied during Japan's last major offensive in China in 1944.

Mao Tse-tung addressing a crowd in November 1944; the war against Japan helped bring about, in 1949, the creation of the People's Republic of China.

The success of Chinese troops against the Japanese, under the command of the US general Joseph Stilwell, only confirmed Chiang Kai-shek's ineffectiveness. Both Stilwell and Chiang Kai-shek were supplied from India, with US and British pilots flying over a series of mountain ridges to make the supply drops. As a result this route was nicknamed the Hump. The awful human cost of China's fight against Japan often tends to be forgotten in accounts of World War II. The number of Chinese nationalists who died fighting, and civilians who died through starvation and disease, is impossible to calculate but it certainly reaches into the millions.

General Slim's 14th Army, composed of British, Indian, Burmese, Chinese and African soldiers, advances towards Mandalay in Burma in March 1945.

'I DID IT FOR MY MOTHERLAND!'

Uno Shintaro, fighting in China, recalls a young Chinese prisoner called Cheng Jing who was proved to have stolen some guns: '... *He was only sixteen or seventeen. He looked so innocent and naïve that they brought him back without killing him. He soon learned our Japanese songs and some officers put him to work in the regimental armoury repairing weapons. Everyone trusted him.*

The regiment received twenty to thirty pistols each year. That year they went missing. Cheng Jing had stolen them and passed them along to the guerrillas ... When he realized he wouldn't be spared, his attitude changed ... As Cheng Jing passed by the door of my room on the way to his execution, he shouted at me, "I will avenge myself on you! I did it for my motherland!"'

[From *Japan At War*, Haruko Taya Cook and Theodore F. Cook]

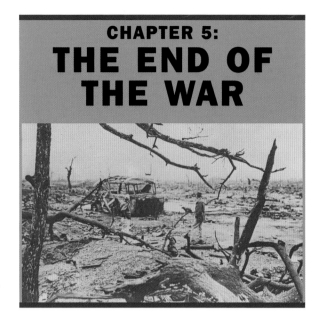

CHAPTER 5:
THE END OF THE WAR

The city of Hiroshima flattened to the ground as the result of a single atomic bomb.

A mushroom cloud over Nagasaki, a result of the atom bomb dropped on the city: 'When you deal with a beast you have to treat him as a beast,' wrote President Truman after the attack.

It was the possibility of Nazi Germany developing an atomic bomb that led to the United States developing its own weapon of mass destruction. When the new bomb was ready, it was used against Japan instead. Plans for the invasion of Japan, with its anticipated high costs in life, supplies and money, were no longer needed once the new type of bomb had been dropped on the cities of Hiroshima and Nagasaki. On 14 August, Japan's Emperor Hirohito announced on Japanese radio that the country had been defeated. Japan surrendered, bringing the Pacific War and World War II to an end.

The use of the atomic bomb remains probably the most controversial issue of the war, although it aroused no great disagreement in 1945. As it turned out, the long-term consequences of the use of the atom bomb were profound. It was the beginning of a horrific change in human history because the world would soon have to live with the fact that nuclear weapons could destroy civilization itself. Some of the scientists involved in the development of the atom bomb realized this and did not want the new weapon to be used. They were overruled, however, because the need to defeat the Japanese was seen as the priority.

HARRY S. TRUMAN Harry S. Truman, the president of the United States at the time, had been informed that between 25,000 and 46,000 Americans

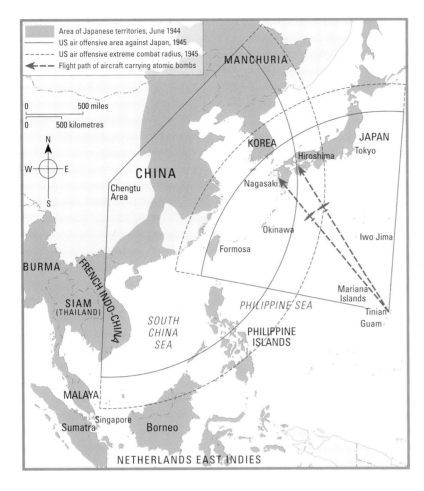

Area of Japanese territories, June 1944
US air offensive area against Japan, 1945
US air offensive extreme combat radius, 1945
Flight path of aircraft carrying atomic bombs

0   500 miles
0   500 kilometres

From Tinian, one of the Mariana Islands captured in the course of 1944, B-29 bombers took off to drop atomic bombs on Hiroshima and Nagasaki.

were likely to die in an invasion of Japan. These lives were saved by the use of the bomb. Countless numbers of Japanese would also have died if the war had been prolonged. It has since been argued that lives could have been saved on both sides if surrender terms had been negotiated before using the bomb. Japanese military leaders knew their country was defeated and attempts to negotiate a peace had already begun. What prevented a peace settlement was the fear that the Emperor, who at the time was regarded as a god, would be dethroned if Japan surrendered unconditionally. If it had been agreed that the Emperor could continue to rule, as he was allowed to after 1945, then a negotiated surrender might have taken place. It is also argued that the US knew that a confrontation with the USSR would occur after the war, and the use of the new weapon was intended to demonstrate the United States' superior power.

When the Pacific War was over, a tribunal was set up in Tokyo to punish those found guilty of war crimes. Twenty-five Japanese leaders were put on trial, resulting in executions and long terms of imprisonment. Around 3,000 other individuals were found guilty in other war crimes trials that took place in the Pacific region; 920 were executed. Emperor Hirohito

ATOMIC BOMBS: THE FACTS

Date:	6 August 1945
Time:	8.15 am
Target of atomic bomb:	Hiroshima city, population: 350,000
Type of atomic bomb:	Uranium
Bomb's nickname:	'Little Boy'
Length of bomb:	3 metres
People killed:	140,000
Date:	9 August 1945
Time:	11.02 am
Target of atomic bomb:	Nagasaki city, population: 270,000
Type of atomic bomb:	Plutonium
Bomb's nickname:	'Fat Man'
Length of bomb:	3.5 metres
People killed:	73,884

Officials representing the Japanese government arrive on the battleship USS *Missouri* to sign surrender terms on 2 September 1945; the Pacific War was finally over.

and many members of his family were granted immunity because the United States wanted to avoid the widespread opposition to their occupation of Japan after 1945 that Hirohito's trial would have created. This decision has been criticized, as has the fact that those running the trials all came from countries that had suffered at the hands of Japan in the war. One of the judges (there were no juries) was a survivor of the Bataan death march and could hardly be impartial.

The long-term consequences of the Pacific War were huge. In China, civil war between Chiang Kai-shek's forces and communists under Mao Tse-tung led in 1949 to the creation of the Communist People's Republic of China. In the last week of the war the USSR declared war on Japan, as the Allies had earlier agreed, and invaded northern Korea. This led to an agreed division of the country, with the north under the influence of the USSR and the south under US influence. Within five years of the end of the war, hostilities erupted between north and south, and Korea became a major theatre of war in the Cold War between the USSR and the USA.

Perhaps the most important long-term consequence was the way in which the Pacific War ended the supremacy of European colonial powers in Asia. In Vietnam, nationalist and communist forces opposing the Japanese were not willing to accept the return of their French colonial masters. The French eventually withdrew and the stage was set for American intervention and the Vietnam War. The Dutch too gave up any attempt to retain their colonial possessions and the state of Indonesia emerged. India, Burma, Malaya and Singapore were also to gain their independence from the British. The map of Asia had changed and the US had emerged as the major power in the Pacific.

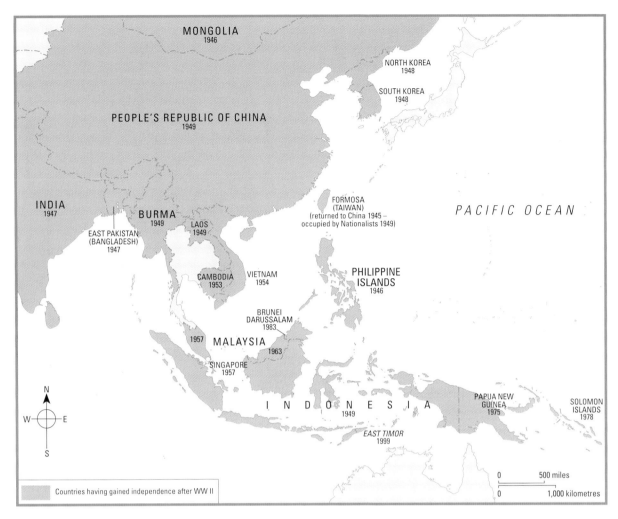

A map showing countries that gained independence after the war. Comparing this map with the one on page 5 shows some of the great changes brought about by the Pacific War. East Asia changed enormously.

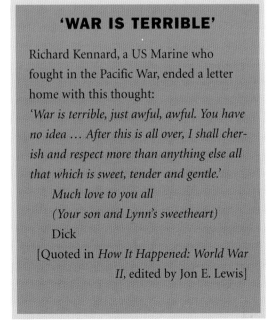

'WAR IS TERRIBLE'

Richard Kennard, a US Marine who fought in the Pacific War, ended a letter home with this thought:

'War is terrible, just awful, awful. You have no idea … After this is all over, I shall cherish and respect more than anything else all that which is sweet, tender and gentle.'

> *Much love to you all*
> *(Your son and Lynn's sweetheart)*
> Dick

[Quoted in *How It Happened: World War II*, edited by Jon E. Lewis]

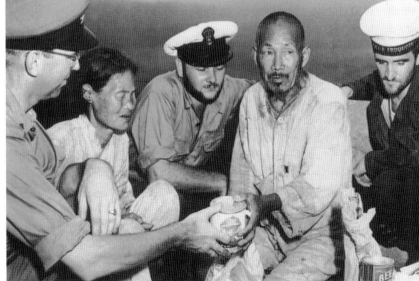

Food rations being dispensed by servicemen to Japanese civilians at the end of the Pacific War.

PROFILES OF MILITARY AND POLITICAL LEADERS

CHIANG KAI-SHEK (1877-1975)

Leader of Chinese nationalists fighting the Japanese after their invasion of China. He was opposed by Mao Tse-tung, the leader of Communist nationalists who were also fighting the Japanese. Chiang Kai-shek was defeated in the civil war between the two sides that resumed after 1945.

WINSTON SPENCER CHURCHILL (1874-1965)

Prime Minister of Great Britain 1940-45. Churchill had little choice but to accept US leadership in the conduct of the Pacific War, especially after the surrender of British land forces to the Japanese in Singapore. Churchill was a keen supporter of the value of his country's empire. He hoped to restore British influence in southeast Asia after the war and maintain the British empire. In this aim, he was not successful.

ADMIRAL WILLIAM HALSEY (1882-1959)

Early in the Pacific War, Halsey was the commander of an aircraft carrier. His ability and willingness to take the offensive contributed to the success of the Guadalcanal campaign and he was promoted because of this. He was very well liked and admired for his tough approach. His conduct at the battle of Leyte Gulf did, however, lead to criticism of his ability to handle a major campaign.

HIROHITO (1901-1989)

Emperor of Japan from 1926 until his death. There is controversy regarding Hirohito's degree of responsibility for bringing Japan into the war. In 1945, many people regarded him as a war leader

who ought to be put on trial and punished. The fact that he was not prosecuted after the war is something that historians still do not agree about. There is evidence, however, that suggests he opposed the military leaders in 1941 but that he could not prevent them from pursuing an aggressive policy that led to the attack on Pearl Harbor. Hirohito played an important role in bringing about the surrender of Japan in 1945.

GENERAL MASAHARU HOMMA (1887-1946)

Japanese army officer who captured the Philippines from the forces of Douglas MacArthur. The campaign, however, took longer than had been planned and Homma was recalled to Japan in August 1942. He remained unemployed for the rest of the war but in 1946 he was put on trial for war crimes committed by his soldiers. Homma claimed that he was unaware of what had happened on the Bataan death march but he was found guilty and executed.

MAJOR-GENERAL CURTIS E. LEMAY (1906-1990)

One of the younger US generals, largely responsible for the air offensive against Japan in 1945. He changed the tactic of high-level precision attacks and adopted a policy of low-level incendiary bombing.

GENERAL DOUGLAS MACARTHUR (1880-1964)

Supreme Allied Commander of the South West Pacific Command during the Pacific War. A controversial leader, MacArthur is regarded by historians as very fortunate to have escaped blame for the defence of the Philippines that resulted in the US defeat. When ordered to escape to Australia in 1942, he famously declared 'I shall return', refusing the suggestion from the US Office of War Information that he should

change the phrase to 'We shall return'. MacArthur, very effective in using the 'island-hopping' approach to bypass pockets of strong Japanese resistance, recaptured the Philippines in 1944. If a land invasion of Japan had been necessary, MacArthur would have been the ground commander for the operation. In the Korean War, MacArthur successfully led the US forces but he lost the command when he tried to continue the war against China.

MAO TSE-TUNG (1893-1976)

A founding member of the Chinese Communist Party in 1921, Mao had risen to lead the Party by the time of the Pacific War. He effectively opposed Chiang Kai-shek by dealing with corruption and social issues, and gained support as a nationalist by fighting the Japanese. By 1945, Mao and his troops had gained control over most of the Chinese countryside. Four years later, he declared the independence of the People's Republic of China.

ADMIRAL CHESTER W. NIMITZ (1885-1966)

Commander-in-Chief US Pacific Fleet and Pacific Ocean Areas during the Pacific War. He was overshadowed to some extent by the more flamboyant MacArthur, though he is regarded as possessing far sounder military judgement. Nimitz planned the battle of Midway and chose to act on the information provided by US intelligence deciphering Japanese radio messages. At this early stage in the war, the value of such intelligence reports was not taken for granted.

Nimitz commanded the landings on Iwo Jima and Okinawa, and signed the Japanese surrender document on behalf of the United States.

FRANKLIN D. ROOSEVELT (1882-1945)

President of the United States at the time of the attack on Pearl Harbor, Roosevelt died in April 1945 and so did not live to see the surrender of Japan. Roosevelt is credited for his leadership in uniting his country in the war against Nazi Germany and Japan. Historians have recognized Roosevelt's ability to manage two separate wars successfully, one in Europe and one in the Pacific. Roosevelt is also seen to have realized that relations with the USSR would be difficult once the war was finally over.

GENERAL SIR WILLIAM SLIM (1891-1970)

British commander in charge of the defence of Imphal in 1944 and of the campaign that drove the Japanese out of Burma in 1945. He once said 'I must have been the most defeated general in our history', but historians have given him great credit for his tactics and his ability to command troops and win the loyalty of soldiers.

ADMIRAL RAYMOND A. SPRUANCE (1886-1969)

A commander at the battle of Midway, Spruance also took part in the battle of the Philippine Sea and the Okinawa campaign. He also planned the capture of Tarawa and the Marshall islands. The US Navy's official historian praised his 'power of decision and coolness in action'.

GENERAL JOSEPH STILWELL (1883-1946)

A US army commander in the China-Burma-India theatre of war who became well known for his harsh criticisms of Chiang Kai-shek. Stilwell, who spoke Chinese fluently, was very successful as a commander of Chinese troops. He gained admiration and promotion for the way he handled his troops and conducted a difficult campaign. Stilwell was also renowned for his inability to get along with British military commanders.

GENERAL HIDEKI TOJO (1884-1948)

Prime Minister of Japan between 1941 and 1944. Before 1941, Tojo was known for his hard-line attitude towards the US and his willingness to adopt a military solution to political problems. When he became Prime Minister in 1941, many observers sensed that it was only a matter of time before Japan was led into a war. After the war, Tojo was convicted of war crimes and hanged.

HARRY S. TRUMAN (1884-1972)

Vice-President of the United States for 83 days, until the death of Roosevelt in April 1945 made Truman the President. He did not know about the programme to build atomic weapons but, guided by Roosevelt's advisers, he made no major changes in military policy.

ADMIRAL ISOROKU YAMAMOTO (1884-1943)

Commander of the Japanese Combined Fleet 1939-43. Yamamoto had lived in the United States in order to learn English and in the 1930s he was opposed to people like Tojo who favoured war with America. When the prospect of war became certain, Yamamoto became convinced that only a surprise attack on Pearl Harbor would give his country a chance of success. Yamamoto, convincing those who thought his plan was a reckless one,

worked out the plan for attacking the US fleet. He also planned the strategy that led to the battle of Midway. Yamamoto was killed by US forces when his aircraft was intercepted and shot down.

GENERAL TOMOYUKI YAMASHITA (1885-1946)

Commander of Japanese forces that conquered Malaya and Singapore, and the commander responsible for the defence of Luzon in the Philippines. After the war, he was put on trial for war crimes committed against civilians in Manila. Yamashita was not responsible for these crimes but he was found guilty and sentenced to death. MacArthur refused to consider his appeal and Yamashita was hanged.

SEPTEMBER 1931
Japan invades Manchuria.

AUGUST 1937
Japan invades China.

3 SEPTEMBER 1939
Britain, France, Australia and India declare war on Nazi Germany.

15 MAY 1940
Dutch (Netherlands) army surrenders to Nazi Germany.

24 JULY 1941
Japanese troops begin occupying French-controlled Indo-China.

26 JULY 1941
US freezes all Japanese assets.

1 AUGUST 1941
US announces oil embargo against Japan; Britain and Netherlands East Indies soon do the same.

7-8 DECEMBER 1941
Japanese troops land in Malaya and Siam (Thailand). Attack on Pearl Harbor. The Philippines and Singapore bombed.

9 DECEMBER 1941
Australia and New Zealand declare war on Japan.

10 DECEMBER 1941
HMS *Prince of Wales* and *Repulse* sunk off coast of Malaya. Japanese troops land in the Philippines.

14 DECEMBER 1941
Japanese begin invasion of Burma.

17 DECEMBER 1941
Japanese invade North Borneo.

20 DECEMBER 1941
Japanese invade Netherlands East Indies (Indonesia).

25 DECEMBER 1941
Japanese invade and capture Hong Kong.

9 JANUARY 1942
Following the capture of Manila by the Japanese, the siege of Bataan begins.

23 JANUARY 1942
Japanese land on Solomon Islands.

25 JANUARY 1942
Defending forces in Malaya ordered to withdraw to island of Singapore.

15 FEBRUARY 1942
Singapore surrenders.

7 MARCH 1942
Japanese land in New Guinea.

11 MARCH 1942
General MacArthur leaves Philippines for Australia.

7 APRIL 1942
US and Filipino troops surrender on Bataan.

18 APRIL 1942
Doolittle bombing raid on Tokyo and other cities in Japan. Sixteen USAAF B-25 bombers under the command of Colonel James Doolittle launched from the aircraft carrier USS *Hornet* operating off the coast of Japan.

6 MAY 1942
Corregidor island falls to the Japanese.

7-8 MAY 1942
Battle of the Coral Sea.

4-5 JUNE 1942
Battle of Midway.

7-8 AUGUST 1942
First US landings on Guadalcanal. Naval battle of Savo Island.

27 SEPTEMBER 1942
Japanese advance on Port Moresby halted.

12-13 NOVEMBER 1942
Naval battle of Guadalcanal begins.

21 JANUARY 1943
Japanese base at Gona, New Guinea, captured and Sananada Point cleared.

9 FEBRUARY 1943
Last Japanese troops begin to leave Guadalcanal.

20 JUNE 1943
US troops land on New Georgia.

15 AUGUST 1943

US landings on Vella Lavella.

6-7 OCTOBER 1943

Japanese evacuate Vella Lavella.

20 NOVEMBER 1943

US landings on Tarawa and
Bougainville.

30 JANUARY 1944

US troops land on Marshall Islands.

17 FEBRUARY 1944

Eniwetok Atoll attacked and
secured by US forces.

8 MARCH 1944

Japanese offensive from Burma into
India begins.

22 APRIL 1944

MacArthur's forces land in New
Guinea.

15 JUNE 1944

Americans land on Saipan.
Strategic bombing campaign
against Japan begins.

19 JUNE 1944

Battle of the Philippine Sea

9 JULY 1944

Saipan secured.

18 JULY 1944

Japanese defeated at Imphal, India.

21-24 JULY 1944

US landings on Guam and Tinian.

15 SEPTEMBER 1944

US landings on Peleliu.

24 OCTOBER 1944

US landings at Leyte, Philippines.
Battle of Leyte Gulf.

9 JANUARY 1945

US forces land on Luzon.

FEBRUARY 1945

Battle for Manila in the Philippines
begins.

19 FEBRUARY 1945

US forces land on Iwo Jima.

3 MARCH 1945

Manila captured.

9 MARCH 1945

First fire-bomb attack on Tokyo.

20 MARCH 1945

British-led troops secure Mandalay
in Burma.

26 MARCH 1945

Fighting ends on Iwo Jima.

1 APRIL 1945

US troops land on Okinawa.

12 APRIL 1945

Truman becomes US President after
the death of Roosevelt.

3 MAY 1945

Allied troops capture Rangoon in
Burma.

6 AUGUST 1945

Atomic bomb dropped on
Hiroshima.

8 AUGUST 1945

USSR declares war on Japan.

9 AUGUST 1945

Atomic bomb dropped on
Nagasaki.

14 AUGUST 1945

Japanese emperor broadcasts to the
country, accepting surrender.

2 SEPTEMBER 1945

Formal Japanese surrender signed
aboard USS *Missouri* in Tokyo Bay.

3 MAY 1946

Tokyo war crimes tribunal begins.

14-15 AUGUST 1947

India becomes independent.

12 JUNE 1948

Armed struggle against the British
in Malaya for independence.

1 OCTOBER 1949

Mao Tse-tung declares Communist
People's Republic of China.

31 DECEMBER 1949

Formal surrender of Dutch control
over Indonesia.

SEPTEMBER 1951

American-led occupation of Japan
ends.

STATISTICS CONCERNING COMBATANT NATIONS

Casualties of the Pacific War

Australia: Over 17,000 deaths; 14,000 wounded.

China: An estimated five million military casualities (killed and wounded); civilian casualties estimated between 10 and 20 million.

India: Over 24,000 deaths in military action; an estimated three million civilian deaths as a result of war-related famine in 1943.

Great Britain: 30,000 deaths; number of wounded unknown.

Japan: 1.8 million deaths in military action; 500,000 civilians killed.

USA: 80,000 deaths; number of wounded unknown.

It is difficult to estimate the number of civilians killed in the course of the war but in total many millions, in the Netherlands East Indies, the Pacific Islands, the Philippines, Burma, Malaya and Korea, died as a result of Japanese occupation and military engagements in their countries.

Principal Combatant Nations

Australia: After Pearl Harbor and the invasion of Malaya, Australia declared war on Japan in December 1941.

China: Invaded by Japanese in 1937, though a region in the north of the country, Manchuria, had been invaded six years earlier. The China Incident, as the Japanese called their fighting there, became part of the Pacific War, and part of World War II as a whole, after the attack on Pearl Harbor in 1941.

Great Britain: Britain and Japan were at war after the Japanese invasion of Malaya in 1941. Britain was already a combatant nation in World War II, having declared war on Nazi Germany in September 1939.

Japan: Japan was at war with China from 1937. After the attack on Pearl Harbor and the invasion of the British colony of Malaya, both occurring at the end of 1941, Japan was at war with the USA and Britain.

USA: After the Japanese attack on Pearl Harbor in December 1941, the USA and Japan were at war.

US Warships Completed or Obtained between July 1940 and September 1945

Battleships	10
Aircraft carriers	27
Escort carriers	111
Cruisers	47
Destroyers	370
Destroyer escorts	504
Submarines	217
Minecraft	975
Patrol ships and craft	1,915
Auxiliary ships	1,612
Landing ships and craft	66,055

Japanese Naval Strength on 7 December 1941

	Existing strength	Under construction
Battleships	10	2
Aircraft carriers	10	4
Cruisers	38	4
Destroyers	112	12
Submarines	65	29
Others	156	88

Comparison of Japanese and US Military Production Figures

	1939	1940	1941	1942	1943	1944	1945
Aircraft USA	5,856	12,804	26,277	47,836	85,898	96,318	49,761
Aircraft Japan	4,467	4,768	5,088	8,861	16,693	28,180	11,066
Tanks USA	–	400	4,052	24,997	29,497	17,565	11,968
Tanks Japan	–	1,023	1,024	1,191	790	401	142
Major naval vessels USA	–	–	544	1,854	2,654	2,247	1,513
Major naval vessels Japan	21	30	49	68	122	248	51

Far East War Crimes Trials: Verdicts and Sentences

Count	1	27	29	31	32	33	35	36	54	55	Sentence
Araki Sadao	G	G	A	A	A	A	A	A	A	A	Life imprisonment
Doihara Kenjiō	G	G	G	G	G	A	G	G	G	O	Hanging
Hashimoto Kingorō	G	G	A	A	A				A	A	Life imprisonment
Hata Shunroku	G	G	G	G	G	A	A	G	A	A	Life imprisonment
Hiranuma Kiichirō	G	G	G	G	G	A	A	G	A	A	Hanging
Hirota Kōki	G	G	A	A	A	A	A		A	G	Life imprisonment
Hoshino Naoki	G	G	G	G	G	A	A		A	A	Life imprisonment
Itagaki Seishirō	G	G	G	G	G	A	G	G	G	O	Hanging
Kaya Okinori	G	G	G	G	G				A	A	Life imprisonment
Kido Koichi	G	G	G	G	G	A	A	A	A	A	Life imprisonment
Kimura Heitarō	G	G	G	G	G				G	G	Hanging
Koiso Kuniaki	G	G	G	G	G			A	A	G	Life imprisonment
Matsui Iwane	A	A	A	A	A		A	A	A	G	Hanging
Minami Jirō	G	G	A	A	A				A	A	Life imprisonment
Mutō Akira	G	G	G	G	G	A		A	G	G	Hanging
Oka Takasumi	G	G	G	G	G				A	A	Life imprisonment
Oshima Hiroshi	G	A	A	A	A				A	A	Life imprisonment
Satō Kenryō	G	G	G	G	G				A	A	Life imprisonment
Shigemitsu Mamoru	A	G	G	G	G	G	A		A	G	7 years imprisonment
Shiimada Shigetarō	G	G	G	G	G						Life imprisonment
Shiratori Toshio	G	A	A	A	A						Life imprisonment
Suzuki Teiichi	G	G	G	G	G		A	A	A	A	Life imprisonment
Tōgō Shigenori	G	G	G	G	G			A	A	A	20 years imprisonment
Tōjō Hideki	G	G	G	G	G	G		A	G	O	Hanging
Umezo Yoshijirō	G	G	G	G	G	G		A	A	A	Life imprisonment

Key

Blank: Not accused of this count. G: Guilty. A: Acquitted (not guilty). O: Charged but no verdict reached.

Count 1:   Overall conspiracy to wage war against 'international law, treaties, agreements or assurances'
Count 27:   Waging war against China
Count 29:   Waging war against the United States
Count 31:   Waging war against the British Commonwealth
Count 32:   Waging war against the Netherlands
Count 33:   Waging war against France
Count 35:   Waging war against the USSR at Lake Khassan
Count 36:   Waging war against the USSR at Nomonhan
Count 54:   Ordering, authorizing, or permitting atrocities
Count 55:   Disregard of duty to secure observance of and prevent breaches of Laws of War

aircraft carrier A large ship with a flight deck from which aircraft may take off and land.

Allies The countries at war against Germany, Japan and their supporters.

atoll A ridge of coral rock and sand, just above the level of the sea, enclosing an area of sea.

banzai A form of greeting, traditionally used by the Japanese to their emperor. A term also used to describe an open, near-suicidal charge by Japanese soldiers against an enemy.

battalion A military formation, made up of an average of around 750 men, under the command of a Lieutenant Colonel.

battleship The largest and most heavily-armed type of warship.

campaign A series of military operations in a particular theatre of war.

civilians People who are not part of the armed forces of a navy, army or air force.

Cold War The period of international tension between 1945 and 1991 when a high level of distrust existed between the USA and the USSR.

colonial Relating to a colony.

colony A country ruled and inhabited by people who represent a foreign government.

conscripted Compelled to join the armed forces.

convoy A group of merchant ships (or other vehicles) travelling together for mutual protection.

cruiser A warship that is less heavily armed than a battleship but which has greater speed.

destroyer A warship used to attack enemy shipping with torpedoes and to protect its own fleet from attack by surface warships and submarines.

division A military formation made up of an average of around 12,000 men, although Japanese divisions were as large as 18,000, under a single command.

emplacement A platform for guns.

evacuate Withdraw from a place, like a scene of battle, often because the situation is considered too dangerous.

exhume Dig out, unearth.

Filipinos People who come from the Philippines.

garrison A fortified position in which troops and their equipment are stationed.

guerrillas Fighters, not part of a regular government army, independently conducting military action.

hypocrites People who are only pretending to be acting for the good.

immunity Freedom from the normal consequences of a law.

impartial Fair, not favouring one side in a dispute.

imperialism A belief in the value of acquiring control over another country's resources and the establishment of colonies, often as part of the controlling country's empire.

imports Goods brought into a country or a region from other countries.

incendiary bombs Bombs designed to create fires rather than to explode.

Indo-China A region of south-east Asia, including modern Vietnam, which was a colony of France before World War II.

intelligence In a military sense, the collecting

of information about the enemy.

interned Placed under a form of imprisonment whereby people are restricted to one place and guarded.

kamikaze Japanese suicide pilots who undertook missions against enemy ships.

killing zone An area where a concentrated amount of killing in the course of a battle takes place.

liberators People who free others from a state of captivity.

Malaya Country in Asia, now called Malaysia, which was a British colony in 1941 when it was overrun by the Japanese.

Manchuria A Chinese state, a territory once disputed by China, Japan and the Soviet Union, occupied by the Japanese in 1931.

marines Soldiers based on warships. Typically marines take part in amphibious operations, landing by sea to engage enemy forces on land.

medic A term for people who provide medical care.

nationalists People who hold strong patriotic beliefs and who are very loyal to the nation state to which they belong.

natural resources Sources of food and fuel, like wheat or oil for example, that belong to a country or region.

Nazi Germany Germany, between 1933 and 1945, when the country was governed by Adolf Hitler and members of his Nazi party.

Netherlands Country in western Europe, also called Holland and its people the Dutch, which lost control over its colonies in Asia after being defeated by Germany in 1940.

Netherlands East Indies Dutch colony in south-east Asia which became Indonesia after it achieved independence after the war.

Niitaka, Mount The highest mountain in Japan, the name of which was used as a code for the attack on Pearl Harbor in 1941.

peninsula A piece of land projecting into the sea and almost surrounded by water.

Philippines The Philippines, made up of thousands of islands and with a population of 17 million in 1941, had been an American colony but was halfway to independence when the Pacific War broke out.

pincer movement An encircling movement by two wings of a force, closing in on the enemy.

Siam Country in Asia, now called Thailand, invaded by the Japanese in 1941.

siege An operation to force a group to surrender by surrounding them and preventing food and support reaching them.

strategy The planning of how military forces are to be used in a military campaign.

supply lines Routes used for providing supplies and weapons during a war.

tactics The planning of how to use military forces when they are in actual contact with the enemy.

task force A unit of people and equipment brought together and organized for a special purpose.

theatre of war A place where a major battle takes place.

traumatic Describes an event that brings about a state of deep emotional shock.

tribunal A court of justice.

unconditional surrender A complete surrender of forces without any prior agreement or terms having been established.

USSR The Union of Soviet Socialist Republics (also known as the Soviet Union), of which Russia was the leading power. It was disbanded at the end of 1991.

RECOMMENDED BOOKS

The following books look at the Pacific War as a whole or look at some of the key episodes in the Pacific War:

Early Sunday Morning: The Pearl Harbor Diary of Amber Billows, Hawaii, 1941, Barry Denenberg (New York, 2001)

Hiroshima, Laurence Yep (New York, 1996)

Hiroshima and Nagasaki, R.G. Grant (London, 1999)

Strategic Battles in the Pacific: World War II, Rice Earle, Jr. (San Diego, 2000)

The World Wars: the War in the Pacific, Peter Chrisp (London, 2003)

Turning Points in History: Pearl Harbor, Richard Tames (London, 2001)

Victory in the Pacific, Julie Klam, Dwight Jon Zimmerman (Mankato, Minnesota, 2003)

World War II in the Pacific, R. Conrad Stein (Berkeley Heights, New Jersey, 2002)

World War II in the Pacific (World History), Don Nardo (San Diego, 2002)

The following books provide interesting and detailed accounts of particular battles or campaigns in the Pacific War:

Atlas of World War II Battle Plans, edited by Stephen Badsey (Oxford, 2000)

Midway: The Japanese Story, Mitsuo Fuchida and Masatake Okumiya (London, 2002)

Peleliu, Jim Moran and Gordon L. Rottman (Oxford, 2002)

Sea Battles in Close-Up: World War 2, Eric Grove (Shepperton, 1993)

Singapore, Alan Warren (London, 2002)

Singapore: The Battle That Changed The War, James Leasor (London, 2001)

Tarawa 1943, Derrick Wright (Oxford, 2000)

Tarawa – A Hell of a Way to Die, Derrick Wright (Marlborough, 1997)

The Battle for Iwo Jima, Derrick Wright (Stroud, 1999)

The following books provide fascinating first-hand accounts by people who experienced the Pacific War, either as combatants or civilians:

How It Happened: World War II, edited by Jon E. Lewis (London, 2002)

Japan At War: An Oral History, Haruko Taya Cook and Theodore F. Cook (London, 2000)

'The Good War': An Oral History of World War II, edited by Studs Terkel (London, 1984)

The following books all provide or include interesting accounts of the Pacific War as a whole, though sometimes there may be too much information for younger readers. In these cases the use of the contents page or index of each book is recommended as a way of finding out more about a particular battle or aspect of the war:

Eagle Against the Sun, Ronald H. Spector (London, 2001)

Hell In The Pacific, Jonathan Lewis and Ben Steele (London, 2001)

The Oxford Companion to World War II, edited by I.C.B. Dear (Oxford, 2001)

The Pacific Campaign, Dan Van Der Vat (Edinburgh, 2001)

The Second World War: The Pacific, David Horner (Oxford, 2002)

The Second World War: A People's History, Joanna Bourke (Oxford, 2001)

SOURCES OF QUOTATIONS

Atlas of World War II Battle Plans, edited by Stephen Badsey (Oxford, 2000)

The *Daily Express* newspaper, (London, 1941)

Hell In The Pacific, Jonathan Lewis and Ben Steele (London, 2001)

How It Happened: World War II, edited by Jon E. Lewis (London, 2002)

Japan At War: An Oral History, Haruko Taya Cook
   and Theodore F. Cook (London, 2000)

Singapore, Alan Warren (London, 2002)

Tarawa – A Hell of a Way to Die, Derrick Wright
   (Marlborough, 1997)

The Battle for Iwo Jima, Derrick Wright (Stroud, 1999)

'The Good War': An Oral History of World War II,
   edited by Studs Terkel (London, 1984)

The Oxford Companion to World War II, edited by
   I.C.B. Dear (Oxford, 2001)

The Pacific Campaign, Dan Van Der Vat (Edinburgh,
   2001)

The Second World War: A People's History, Joanna
   Bourke (Oxford, 2001)

RECOMMENDED VIDEOS

The following films are set in the context of the Pacific
War and are worth watching. They are all available on
video.

Empire of the Sun (1987)

Sands of Iwo Jima (1950)

The Bridge on the River Kwai (1957)

Tora! Tora! Tora! (1970)

The following documentaries about the Pacific War are
also available on video.

Chronicles of World War II, with Walter Cronkite: Vol
   2: *The Pacific War Begins* and Vol 7: *The Pacific
   Campaign* (1981), 20th Century Fox

Hell in the Pacific (2001), Carlton Visual
   Entertainment

*V is for Victory – America Goes to War – Guadalcanal
   and the Pacific Counterattack* (1998), Accord
   Media UK

RECOMMENDED DVDS

The films mentioned above should soon become available on DVD and the documentary *Hell in the Pacific*
is already available on DVD. The following documentary is only available on DVD.

Battle Cry: Objective Burma – Operation Pacific
   (2003), Warner Home Videos

RECOMMENDED WEBSITES

www.combinedfleet.com/map.htm
This website has maps and summaries of naval engagements in the Pacific War.
www.historyplace.com
Click on the World War II tab for battle photographs
of US troops in the Pacific War, a timeline and features
on Pearl Harbor and African-Americans in the war.
www.iwm.org.uk/
The website for the Imperial War Museum in London.
www.nimitz-museum.org/
This is the website for the National Museum of the
Pacific War in the USA.
www.spartacus.schoolnet.co.uk/2WWpacific.htm
This website has a helpful summary of the Pacific War
with lots of useful links along the way.

Note to parents and teachers

Every effort has been made by the publishers to ensure
that these websites are suitable for children; that they
are of the highest educational value; and that they
contain no inappropriate or offensive material.
However, because of the nature of the Internet, it is
impossible to guarantee that the contents of these sites
will not be altered. We strongly advise that Internet
access is supervised by a responsible adult.

PLACES TO VISIT

The National Museum of the Pacific War is the only
institution in the continental United States dedicated
exclusively to telling the story of the Pacific Theatre
battles of World War II. It is located at:
The National Museum of the Pacific War, 340 East
Main Street, Fredericksburg, Texas 78624.

Two other important museums in the United States
are:
The Naval Historical Center, Washington Naval Yard,
Washington D.C. 20374 (www.history.navy.mil)
The USS *Arizona* Visitor Center, Pearl Harbor Naval
Base, Hawaii.
The Imperial War Museum, Lambeth Rd, London, SE1
6HZ, has lots of exhibits relating to World War II as a
whole.

INDEX

Numbers in **bold** refer to captions to pictures or, where indicated, to maps.